2/04

55.00

D0154228

Contemporary
Hispanic Quotations

Contemporary
Hispanic Quotations

Compiled and Edited by
Daniel E. Stanton and Edward F. Stanton

GREENWOOD PRESS
Westport, Connecticut · London

Library of Congress Cataloging-in-Publication Data

Contemporary Hispanic quotations / compiled and edited by Daniel E. Stanton and Edward F. Stanton.
　　p. cm.
Includes bibliographical references and indexes.
ISBN 0–313–31464–0 (alk. paper)
　　1. Hispanic Americans—Quotations, maxims, etc.　2. Hispanic Americans—Quotations.　I. Stanton, Daniel E.　II. Stanton, Edward F., 1942–
PN6084.H47C66 2003
973'.0468—dc21　　　　2002032070

British Library Cataloguing in Publication Data is available.

Library of Congress Catalog Card Number: 2002032070
ISBN: 0–313–31464–0

First published in 2003

Greenwood Press, 88 Post Road West, Westport, CT 06881
An imprint of Greenwood Publishing Group, Inc.
www.greenwood.com

Printed in the United States of America

The paper used in this book complies with the
Permanent Paper Standard issued by the National
Information Standards Organization (Z39.48–1984).

10　9　8　7　6　5　4　3　2　1

To Priscila and Mr. Los

Contents

Acknowledgments

We would like to thank our research assistant, Genny Ballard; Prof. Rolando Hinojosa-Smith, University of Texas, *cuate para siempre;* Rosemarie Kuhn; and Prof. Jaime A. Mejía, Southwest Texas State University.

We would also like to express our special gratitude to all those who generously offered us original quotes for this book: Arturo Arias, María Celeste Arrarás, Judith F. Baca, Rubén Benítez, Manuel Cortés Castañeda, María Antonieta Collins, Celestino Fernández, Juan Carlos Galeano, Dan Guerrero, Rolando Hinojosa-Smith, Francisco Jiménez, Gloria Molina, Linda Montoya, Yanira Paz, Eloy Rodríguez, Enrico Mario Santí, Nicomedes Suárez-Araúz, Gloria Vando, Anita Vélez-Mitchell, Alma Luz Villanueva and José Antonio Villarreal.

Finally, we are grateful to those authors or their agents who have granted us permission to quote passages from their poetry and fiction: Rudolfo Anaya, Gloria Anzaldúa, Ana Castillo, Rolando Hinojosa-Smith and Alma Luz Villanueva.

Introduction

Some thirty-seven million Hispanics reside in the United States, yet this is the first book of its kind dedicated to the country's largest minority population.[1] Our collection offers approximately 1,000 quotations from Hispanic writers, artists, entertainers, politicians, activists, educators, professionals and athletes, among others. Their words cover a vast array of subjects. Writers and artists discuss their inspiration and the problems of working between two languages and cultures; entertainers reveal the stereotypes that still plague the media; politicians, activists and educators document the struggle for acceptance, enfranchisement and equality; professionals and athletes give testimony to the obstacles they have overcome on the way to prominence in their fields. Themes that run throughout the book include racism, the importance of family and religion, the inexhaustible richness of Hispanic culture and the rewards of patience and perseverance. In this way the book constitutes a kind of personal and collective history of modern Hispanic life in the United States. The editors have attempted to choose quotations for their historical accuracy, for the incisiveness and beauty of their words and for their ability to engage the next generation in the dynamics of its culture.

"Hispanic" is a complex word. For the purposes of our collection, the term is interchangeable with "Latino" or "Latina." People described by these words have lived in the United States and trace some or all of their ancestry to Latin America, the Iberian Peninsula or the Philippine Islands. The subjects of our book have roots in the continental United States, Mexico, Puerto Rico, Cuba, the Dominican Republic, Guatemala, El Salvador, Nicaragua, Costa Rica, Panama, Colombia, Venezuela, Peru, Ecuador, Bolivia, Chile, Argentina, Spain, Portugal and the Philippines. *Contemporary Hispanic Quotations* also includes a small number of citations from noteworthy Latin Americans who have not been permanent residents of the

United States but who have received significant recognition from Americans.

In addition to being a complex word, "Hispanic" is also a controversial one. Some prefer another generic term like "Latino" or "Latina"; others use specific words like Chicano or Chicana, Puerto Rican, Cuban American and so on. The editors have used "Hispanic" because it is the most generally accepted of all these terms, and the most inclusive. Unfortunately, at least one well-known writer has refused to permit her work to be included in a book that has the word "Hispanic" in its title.

Our emphasis is contemporary. Most of the people quoted here are alive. Some have been dead for several decades, but in different ways they still make their presence felt. César Chávez, Roberto Clemente and Rita Hayworth, for example, remain icons of American and Hispanic life, both in the United States and throughout the world.

Our collection of quotations is distinguished from others by passages from fiction and poetry. *Bartlett's*, the classic dictionary of quotes, made its reputation as a compendium of citations drawn mostly from literary works, and we have modestly followed its example. Another original feature of the book is the section of proverbs and popular sayings that reflect the Hispanic community's lively oral tradition. "Anonymous Graffiti, Quotations and Proverbs" appears at the end of the alphabetical list of sources.[2]

Our book does not rely on printed sources only; it also contains original statements offered expressly for *Contemporary Hispanic Quotations*. In a few cases we have included words from radio, television and other nonprint sources.[3] We have translated some quotations from Spanish to English. Unless stated otherwise, the editors have done all translations.

Many of the people quoted in this book are not public figures whose vital facts are readily accessible. On the other hand, some public figures have refused to disclose personal information. For these reasons, we have not been able to record the age or place of birth of some Hispanics whose quotations appear in the book. We welcome additions and corrections for possible reprintings.

How to Use *Contemporary Hispanic Quotations*

All quotations are arranged alphabetically by the authors' names. Readers should note that many Hispanics use two last names: first their father's, then their mother's maiden name. An example would be the writer Rolando Hinojosa-Smith, whose father's last name was Hinojosa and his mother's Smith. In these cases, which are the great majority, the individual will be listed according to the first or paternal last name: H for Hinojosa-Smith in our example. In contrast, a few Hispanics consider their second last name to be primary, whether it is their mother's maiden name or their husband's last name. An example would be the writer Judith Ortiz Cofer. These individuals will be listed under their second last name: C for Cofer.

For any given person, the quotations are arranged chronologically.

At the end of the book, readers will find, in addition to "Anonymous Graffiti, Quotations and Proverbs" (appendix I), "Fields of Professional Activity" (appendix II), an author index and a subject and key word Index.

NOTES

1. Estimated by the U.S. Census Bureau, January 2003.

2. The work and advice of Prof. Shirley Arora (University of California, Los Angeles), an authority on Mexican proverbs, has been very helpful for this section.

3. See quotations by Richard Rodríguez, Carlos Santana and Esmeralda Santiago in the text. One quote by singer Celia Cruz derives from an honorary degree announcement posted at the University of Miami (1999); one by Bishop Patrick Flores reproduces a banner displaying his motto at his consecration (1970); one by drummer Tito Puente was pronounced live in concert at the Blue Note in New York City (1998); and another was heard in a "phone play" by José Rivera at the Humana Festival of New American Plays in Louisville, Kentucky (2000).

Quotations

A

Kirk Acevedo (New York, New York, 1972)

A Puerto Rican American from New York City, Kirk Acevedo has become well known in his role as Miguel Álvarez, head of a Latino prison gang in the television show *Oz*. He has also appeared in films.

> People are seeing you as a character and not a person doing a character. That's the great thing about being an actor.
>
> *Latina* (November 1998)

Iván Acosta (1943)

Iván Acosta is the author of *El Súper* (1982), the most successful Spanish-language play ever produced in the United States. The play was converted into a prize-winning movie directed by León Ichaso.

> I don't know what in the devil you are looking for in Miami. The people there haven't progressed, they still live in 1959, in the "Cuba of yesterday." . . . What you're going to make is a trip into the past. Make your trips and let me make mine. Here, here is where the action is.
>
> *El Súper* (1982)

Marjorie Agosín (Bethesda, Maryland, 1955)

Born in the United States but raised in Chile until she was fifteen, poet and writer Marjorie Agosín studied at the University of Georgia and Indiana University. She has published several collections of poetry and writes book reviews for the *Boston Globe, Christian Science Monitor* and *New York Times*. Agosín has been a member of the advisory board of *Ms.* magazine. She teaches at Wellesley College in Massachusetts.

My writing is linked to the speech of those who do not speak.
Diane Telgen and Jim Kamp (eds.), *Notable Hispanic American Women* (1993)

Christina Aguilera (Staten Island, New York, 1980)

Teen-pop singer Christina Aguilera started her career at the age of eight. She recorded the song "Reflection" for the soundtrack of the animated movie *Mulan* in 1998 and released her first album the following year. In 2000 she won a Grammy Award for the best new artist.

I am fearless. I'm more afraid of the little things than of the bigger things.
New York Times (September 6, 1999)

I'm half Irish, half Latina. My father's from Ecuador. I've never been there or to Ireland—that'd be cool. I want to see the whole world.
YM (Young and Modern) (January 2000)

When I see all these people screaming and chanting and holding signs that they make just for me, my eyes light up, my whole body lifts, and I feel like I'm in another state, I'm floating on air.
YM (Young and Modern) (January 2000)

[On winning a Grammy Award in 2000] Omigod, you guys, I seriously do not have a speech prepared whatsoever.
Grammy (Spring/Summer 2000)

Jessica Alba (Pomona, California, 1981)

The star of Fox's sci-fi television series *Dark Angel*, Jessica Alba has Spanish, Italian, Danish and Canadian roots.

Guys are visually stimulated. They're easy to manipulate. All you have to do is dress up in a sexy outfit. Girls just have this power over guys. Guys are sort of stupid that way.
Entertainment Weekly (March 16, 2001)

Most women have it [the power over men], but once you start to abuse it—once you start to manipulate people with it—you become lame. It's no longer a power but a fault. The secret to using that power is not to use it. Just having it is enough.
Entertainment Weekly (March 16, 2001)

Luis Alfaro (Los Angeles, California)

A writer/performer who works in theater, poetry, fiction and journalism, Luis Alfaro grew up in the Pico-Union district, an impoverished Latino neighborhood in downtown Los Angeles. He has also been a director, producer, curator and community organizer. Alfaro is the author of *Down-*

town (1990) and many other plays. He has been selected as one of the "100 Coolest People" by *Buzz* magazine and recently won a "genius grant" from the MacArthur Foundation.

> *Ay Mijo* [my son], don't you see? Blood is thicker than water, family is greater than friends, and the Virgin Mary watches over all of us.
>
> *Downtown* (1990)

Isabel Allende (Lima, Peru, 1942)

Since the military coup in Chile that killed her uncle Salvador Allende, novelist Isabel Allende has lived outside of her country. She is probably the most famous writer in Spanish now living in the United States. Her works include *The House of the Spirits* (1983), *Of Love and Shadows* (1984), *Eva Luna* (1987), *Paula* (1994) and *Aphrodite: A Memoir of the Senses* (1998). Some of her recent books have been written in English.

Isabel Allende. Photo by Jerry Bauer. Courtesy of Photofest.

My husband, who is a lawyer, is very careful with words and with the truth. He thinks that the truth exists, and it's something that is beyond questioning, which I think is totally absurd. I have several versions of how we met and how wonderful he was and all that. At least twenty. And I'm sure that they are all true. He has one. And I'm positive that it's not true.

> Naomi Epel, *Writers Dreaming* (1993)

I repent of my diets, the delicious dishes rejected out of vanity, as much as I lament the opportunities for making love that I let go by because of pressing tasks or puritanical virtue.

> *New York Times* (April 25, 1998)

They [Hispanics] come here to do the kind of work that an American will never do. You will not be able to stop them. They will integrate. Sooner or later, their children will be with the white children in the schools. It's unavoidable: in 20 years they will be part of this society, just as the Jews are, the Irish, everybody.

> *Mother Jones Interactive* (December 1999)

The biggest straitjacket is all the prejudices that we carry around, and all the fears. But what if we just surrender to the fear? There are things greater than fear. The great, wonderful quality of human beings is that we can overcome even absolute terror, and we do.

> *Mother Jones Interactive* (December 1999)

We [Hispanics] carry with us the sense that we belong to a group, a clan, a tribe, an extended family, especially a country. Whatever happens to you happens to the collective group, and you can never leave behind the past. What you have done in your life will always be with you. So, for us, we have the burden of this sort of fate, of destiny, that you [North Americans] don't.

> *Mother Jones Interactive* (December 1999)

I live in Marin County [California], where a part of the community is fighting against the Latin American immigrants. People are terrified because they see these dark men standing in groups waiting for someone to offer a job. That's very threatening. Because they don't know them and don't understand their ways or their language, they feel that these men are criminals, that they don't pay their share in this society and yet they benefit. That is not true. They don't pay taxes, but they don't benefit.

> *Mother Jones Interactive* (December 1999)

Néstor Almendros (Barcelona, Spain, 1930–1992)

Raised in Spain and Cuba, Néstor Almendros was an internationally recognized cinematographer for thirty years. He worked with some of the world's greatest directors. Because he spoke out against the abuse of human rights in Cuba, the Néstor Almendros Prize for courage in filmmaking is granted in his name.

> Cinema was like a drug, a way out, and American films were, of course, our staple diet.
>
> Néstor Almendros, *A Man with a Camera* (1980)

> I've had a successful career. I've made forty-seven movies and I've got several awards, and there's a moment when you owe something to society. I have access to camera and film, and I know how. The Cuban case [the Revolution and communism] is too scandalous not to talk about.
>
> *New York Times* (December 2, 1988)

Felipe Alou (Haina, Dominican Republic, 1935)

The second Latino in the major leagues, Felipe Alou played baseball for nineteen years before becoming a manager in 1992. He has proven himself to be one of the greatest motivators in the game. He was named National League Manager of the Year in 1994.

> When I came over here [to the United States] I didn't know English. I was supposed to be a darkie. I had no baseball teaching. I didn't know about the racial encounters that I was going to endure. I didn't know about winter or snow. I survived that. Hundreds of Latins will tell you the same thing.
>
> *Sporting News* (June 21, 1993)

> The only reason we [Hispanics] survived is because we are different. We are survivors. We never give up; we never quit. We quit when we die. That is the spirit of the Latin. We are a hard people to put away.
>
> *Sporting News* (June 21, 1993)

> I joke that I like marriage so much that I got married four times.
>
> *Toronto Globe and Mail* (July 23, 1994)

> My father did three things for me. He bought me a pair of spikes when I was 14, though later he cut off the cleats and wore those shoes to work in his shop because he didn't have any other shoes. He gave me his permission to sign my contract. And he was behind me till the day he died.
>
> *Sports Illustrated* (June 19, 1995)

Alurista (Alberto Baltazar Urista) (Mexico City, Mexico, 1947)

Considered by many to be the poet laureate of Chicano letters, Alurista can move with facility between English, Spanish, Nahuatl and Maya (indigenous languages of Mexico), between standard usage and slang. He is also an activist, psychologist, teacher, founder of Centro Cultural de la Raza and cofounder of Movimiento Estudiantil Chicano de Aztlán (Aztlán Chicano Student Movement; MECHA).

> I don't want to brag, but I believe that I was the first modern Chicano writer who dared send bilingual work to an editor. I remember the reaction of one editor when I first gave him my poetry. He said, "Listen, this is a *pochismo* [Spanglish]. Why can't you write either in Spanish or English? . . . " He said he wouldn't publish trash like that. . . . However, a week later he called me on the telephone and said, "Send me your work because it's going to be a hit." . . . After that, if I'm not mistaken, many Chicano and Chicana writers began to publish bilingually.
>
> Juan Bruce-Novoa, *Chicano Authors: Inquiry by Interview* (1980)

> We have to give ourselves the responsibility of constructing a vision of the world that is truly ours, not a colonized vision of the world. An independent, liberated view of reality. If we paint a more humanistic world to live in, we will construct that world. If we paint a nightmare, we'll live in a nightmare.
>
> Juan Bruce-Novoa, *Chicano Authors: Inquiry by Interview* (1980)

> Even when it comes to the question of writing, I write and read in English and Spanish and I do it very deliberately, I try to read a book in Spanish and one in English.
>
> *Dictionary of Literary Biography*, Vol. 82 (1989)

Anthony Alvarado (Unknown place and date of birth)

Anthony Alvarado is former chancellor of New York City Public Schools and superintendent of a school district in Spanish Harlem.

> You have to reach way into yourself and discover . . . your core that is you . . . [and] you are stronger and you know what you believe in and you don't get so distracted by all the garbage.
>
> *New York Times* (July 18, 1988)

Melba Alvarado (Mayarí, Cuba, 1919)

After spending her first fifteen years in Cuba, activist Melba Alvarado moved with her family to the United States. She has lived the rest of her life in the New York City area, where she founded the annual United Hispanic American Parade. Her work has been recognized by King Juan Carlos of Spain, the Federation of Hispanic Societies and the American Legion.

I've learned to balance two cultures. As a child we kept our Hispanic culture at home. I also love American life, art, and the theater. There have always been two cultures in my life and I always enjoyed them both.

Joseph M. Palmisano (ed.), Notable Hispanic American Women, Book II (1998)

Julia Álvarez (New York, New York, 1950)

Educator and author Julia Álvarez spent most of her childhood in her parents' native country, the Dominican Republic. After an aborted overthrow of the dictator Trujillo in 1960, her family fled to the United States. Álvarez has been a professor of English and creative writing at many institutions and now teaches at Middlebury College. She has received several awards, notably for her best-known novel *How the García Girls Lost Their Accents* (1992).

Although I was raised in the Dominican Republic by Dominican parents in an extended Dominican family, mine was an American childhood.

American Scholar (Winter 1987)

All my childhood I had dressed like an American, eaten American foods, and befriended American children. I had gone to an American school and spent most of the day speaking and reading English. At night, my prayers were full of blond hair and blue eyes and snow.

American Scholar (Winter 1987)

[After her airplane was struck by lightning] In the next seat, at the window, sat a young businessman who had been confidently working. Now he looked worried—something that really worries me: when confident-looking businessmen look worried.

O (Oprah magazine) (November 2000)

[After her airplane was struck by lightning] Among the many feelings going through my head during those excruciating 20 minutes was pride—pride in how well everybody on board was behaving. No one panicked. No one screamed. As we jolted and screeched our way downward, I could hear small pockets of soothing conversation everywhere.

O (Oprah magazine) (November 2000)

[Referring to the time her airplane was struck by lightning] Even now, back on terra firma, walking down a Vermont road, I sometimes hear an airplane and look up at that small, glinting piece of metal. I remember the passengers on that fateful, lucky flight and wish I could thank them for the many acts of kindness I witnessed and received. I am indebted to my fellow passengers and wish I could pay them back.

O (Oprah magazine) (November 2000)

The point is not to pay back kindness but to pass it on.

O (Oprah magazine) (November 2000)

I thought of something I had heard a friend say about the wonderful gift his dying father had given the family: He had died peacefully, as if not to alarm any of them about an experience they would all have to go through someday.

O (Oprah magazine) (November 2000)

I've been working on a story based on an incident that happened to my father when he first came to the United States on a visit in the thirties. He went to use the toilet in a rest stop in New Orleans, and there were two doors marked WHITE and OTHER. His English wasn't so good, so he took the labels literally. He could see he wasn't WHITE; he had olive skin. But he wasn't sure he was OTHER either. My father couldn't remember what he ended up doing, but he didn't think he went in either door.

Hungry Mind Review Web site (2000)

As [French novelist Gustave] Flaubert said, Madame Bovary, c'est moi! We do become our characters; male, female; old, young; Anglo, Latina. But it might just be that the imaginative challenge is greater when we have to cross that autobiographical line and become the opposite gender.

Hungry Mind Review Web site (2000)

My sisters and I were in school, so a combination [of Spanish and English] is what we spoke at home. Spanish with the parents and English with us—not even English. Spanglish. It would be "Where did you put my *secadora* [hair dryer]?"

The Politics of Fiction Web site (2000)

Coming to this country I discovered books, I discovered that it was a way to enter into a portable homeland that you could carry around in your head. You didn't have to suffer what was going on around you. I found in books a place to go.

The Politics of Fiction Web site (2000)

When I went to college, we read a little Jane Austen and Emily Dickinson. Like that was really going to help me, a Latina woman. I love Jane Austen, I love Emily Dickinson, but I thought I had to write like them in order to be a writer in English. I didn't know you could put *amorcito* [a little love] in a story in English. I didn't know you could do that.

The Politics of Fiction Web site (2000)

I am greedy for readers. I bristle when people say I'm just a writer for Latinos, like some sort of sociological thing, like to say Faulkner's just a writer for white Southerner men, because he was a white Southern man. That's again the autobiographical fallacy, just tethering yourself to your little bunch.

The Politics of Fiction Web site (2000)

I write to find out what I'm thinking. I write to find out who I am. I write to understand things.

The Politics of Fiction Web site (2000)

Latino writers stand on the shoulders of the African American writers who paved the way, who with a new voice, a new face and a new rage enriched the canon of American literature.

Black Issues Book Review (March 2001)

Emilio Ambasz (Resistencia, Argentina, 1943)

Architect, inventor and designer Emilio Ambasz studied at Princeton University. Before starting his own company, he was design curator at the Museum of Modern Art in New York City. He holds more than 200 design patents.

The large executive chair elevates the sitter . . . and it is covered with the skin of some animal, preferably your predecessor.

Smithsonian (April 1986)

It is my deep belief that design is an act of invention. I believe that its real task begins once functional and behavioral needs have been satisfied. It is not hunger, but love and fear, and sometimes wonder, which make us create. Our milieu may change from generation to generation, but the task, I believe, remains the same: to give poetic form to the pragmatic.

Publicity materials, Emilio Ambasz & Associates (2001)

Rudolfo A. Anaya (Pastura, New Mexico, 1937)

"Godfather and guru of Chicano literature," Rudolfo Anaya is the author of many books, including the bestselling novel *Bless Me, Ultima* (1972), for which he won the Premio Quinto Sol. He has also won many other awards. Now retired, he was a professor of English at the University of New Mexico.

It was the custom to provide for the old and the sick. There was always room in the safety and warmth of *la familia* for one more person, be that person a stranger or a friend.

Bless Me, Ultima (1972)

Rudolfo Anaya. © Cynthia Farah, 1986. Courtesy of the Center for Southwest Research, General Library, University of New Mexico.

It was sad to see my father cry, but I understood it, because sometimes a man has to cry.

Bless Me, Ultima (1972)

Aleluya! Aleluya! Aleluya! The Holy Mother Church took us under her wings and instructed us in her ways.

Bless Me, Ultima (1972)

Easter and first holy communion! Very little else mattered in my life. School work was dull and uninspiring compared to the mysteries of religion.

Bless Me, Ultima (1972)

I learned much from those men who were as dark and quiet as the earth of the valley, and what I learned made me stronger inside.

Bless Me, Ultima (1972)

This is how we have lived along the river, the *viejos* said. We have raised generations on this earth along the Río Grande, and we have done it with pride and honor. Each new generation must accept the custom and likewise pass it on.

Rudolfo A. Anaya, *Alburquerque* (1992)

Those at the bottom always catch the *caca*.

Rudolfo A. Anaya, *Alburquerque* (1992)

We are *nada* [nothing], and even love dies.

Rudolfo A. Anaya, *Alburquerque* (1992)

Born again on New Mexican chile—it's something these newcomers can't understand, he thought. I can't eat a meal if I don't have a bowl of chile on the side. *Comida sin chile no es comida* [Food without chile peppers is not food], as the Mexicans say.

Rudolfo A. Anaya, *Alburquerque* (1992)

For the Chicano, the roots of the idea of maleness extend not only into the Mediterranean world but also into the Native American world. We still act out patterns of male behavior emerging from those historic streams.

Ray González (ed.), *Muy Macho: Latino Men Confront Their Manhood* (1996)

Drunkenness, abusing women, raising hell (all elements of *la vida loca* [the crazy life]) are some mistaken conceptions of what macho means. And yet the uninformed often point to such behavior and call it machismo. In fact, much of this negative behavior is aped by a new generation, because as young men they are not aware that they are being conditioned. Young men acting contrary to the good of their community have not yet learned the real essence of maleness.

Ray González (ed.), *Muy Macho: Latino Men Confront Their Manhood* (1996)

There is no doubt that this country needs to feel, sense, understand, acknowledge, and care about—I don't mean tolerate—the presence of Hispanics in this country. We get nowhere tolerating. We need to love one another!

anq (American Notes & Queries) (Spring 1997)

Don't just tolerate people, love people. All good flows from that.

anq (American Notes & Queries) (Spring 1997)

The country will be wiser and healthier, when it stops seeing us as the Other and sees us as integral to the land we have lived on for so long. Integral to the history our ancestors created, the stories they brought with them, told, the home life they honored, the faith of their religions, the myth of their many roots, and the richness therein.

anq (American Notes & Queries) (Spring 1997)

As *mestizos,* we have to understand not only our European heritage, but also our Native American heritage. If you only understand part of yourself, you're incomplete.

Hispanic (September 1999)

We not only have a social, economic, political history. We have a my-
thology. We have an oral tradition. We have *cuentos* [stories, folktales].

Hispanic (September 1999)

As *mexicanos* and Chicanos in this country . . . we know we have a
history, an oral tradition, a literature, and that our ancestors taught us
the path that is fulfilling and productive for us. Sometimes, however,
we have gotten lost, especially the young people that are too attracted
by the material world and by, what I like to call, false cultures. They're
in cultures that are not good for their souls, not good for their spirits,
and in many ways not good for their bodies, because they give in to the
violent ways of life.

Hispanic (September 1999)

The communal traditions of one generation are changed by the next,
and we have to accept it and learn how the changes happen, and what
is good or bad about that change. Sometimes you have to break free of
family and community to find a new level of awareness for yourself.

Hispanic (September 1999)

Marc Anthony (New York, New York, 1969)

Born and raised in New York City, Marc Anthony is one of today's most
popular salsa artists. He has won two Billboard Awards and a Grammy
for best tropical-Latin performance. Anthony is also an actor.

To sing came easy to me. Once I knew the physical aspect of it, the only
thing I had to concentrate on was my performance and that's what it's
all about: not just to sing but to perform.

Marc Anthony Online Web site (2000)

It's not my fault to have been born and raised in New York, and I
wouldn't change it for anything in the world because it has contributed
to my being me. But I will go to Puerto Rico for a while, just to get that
feeling.

Marc Anthony Online Web site (2000)

I don't want to do something just for the sake of doing it. I either feel it
or I don't.

Marc Anthony Online Web site (2000)

As for salsa, I definitely want to make a change. I believe my greatest
advantage is that I don't know the music theoretically, I just feel it. . . .
That's how I am going to change things.

Marc Anthony Online Web site (2000)

Gloria Anzaldúa (Jesús María of the Valley, Texas, 1942)

Gloria Anzaldúa calls herself a *tejana,* a Texan of Mexican descent. She is a lesbian-feminist poet and fiction writer who has taught at various universities and won several literary prizes.

One day I will walk through walls, grow wings and fly.
> Cherríe Moraga and Gloria Anzaldúa (eds.), *This Bridge Called My Back. Writings by Radical Women of Color* (1981)

The act of writing is the act of making soul, alchemy. It is the quest for the self, for the center of the self, which we women of color have come to think as "other"—the dark, the feminine.
> Cherríe Moraga and Gloria Anzaldúa (eds.), *This Bridge Called My Back. Writings by Radical Women of Color* (1981)

Forget the room of one's own—write in the kitchen, lock yourself up in the bathroom. Write on the bus or the welfare line, on the job or during meals, between sleeping or waking. I write while sitting on the john.
> Cherríe Moraga and Gloria Anzaldúa (eds.), *This Bridge Called My Back. Writings by Radical Women of Color* (1981)

I say *mujer mágica* [magic woman], empty yourself. Shock yourself into new ways of perceiving the world, shock your readers into the same. Stop the chatter inside their heads.
> Cherríe Moraga and Gloria Anzaldúa (eds.), *This Bridge Called My Back. Writings by Radical Women of Color* (1981)

"Don't go out in the sun," my mother would tell me when I wanted to play outside. "If you get any darker, they'll mistake you for an Indian. And don't get dirt on your clothes. You don't want people to say you're a dirty Mexican." It never dawned on her that, though sixth-generation American, we were still Mexican and that all Mexicans are part Indian.
> Cherríe Moraga and Gloria Anzaldúa (eds.), *This Bridge Called My Back. Writings by Radical Women of Color* (1981)

Guilt lay folded in the tortilla. The Anglo kids laughing—calling us "tortilleros," the Mexican kids taking up the word and using it as a club with which to hit each other. My brothers, sister and I started bringing white bread sandwiches to school. After a while we stopped taking our lunch altogether.
> Cherríe Moraga and Gloria Anzaldúa (eds.), *This Bridge Called My Back. Writings by Radical Women of Color* (1981)

I am a border woman. I grew up between two cultures, the Mexican (with a heavy Indian influence) and the Anglo (as a member of a colonized people in our own territory). I have been straddling that *Tejas*-Mexican border, and others, all my life. It's not a comfortable territory to live in, this place of contradictions. Hatred, anger and exploitation are the prominent features of this landscape.

Gloria Anzaldúa, *Borderlands/La Frontera: The New Mestiza* (1987)

So, don't give me your tenets and your laws. Don't give me your luke-warm gods. What I want is an accounting with all three cultures—white, Mexican, Indian. I want the freedom to carve and chisel my own face, to staunch the bleeding with ashes, to fashion my own gods out of my entrails. And if going home is denied me then I will have to stand and claim my space, making a new culture—*una cultura mestiza*—with my own lumber, my own bricks and mortar and my own feminist architecture.

Gloria Anzaldúa, *Borderlands/La Frontera: The New Mestiza* (1987)

Today, *la Virgen de Guadalupe* is the single most potent religious, political and culture image of the Chicano/*mexicano*. She, like my race, is a syn-thesis of the old world and the new, of the religion and culture of the two races in our psyche, the conquerors and the conquered. She is the symbol of the *mestizo* true to his or her Indian values. *La cultura chicana* identifies with the mother (Indian) rather than with the father (Spanish). Our faith is rooted in indigenous attributes, images, symbols, magic and myth. Because Guadalupe took upon herself the psychological and physical devastation of the conquered and oppressed *indio* [Indian], she is our spiritual, political and psychological symbol. As a symbol of hope and faith, she sustains and insures our survival.

Gloria Anzaldúa, *Borderlands/La Frontera: The New Mestiza* (1987)

Los chicanos, how patient we seem, how very patient. There is the quiet of the Indian about us. We know how to survive. When other races have given up their tongue, we've kept ours. We know what it is to live under the hammer blow of the dominant *norteamericano* [North American] cul-ture. But more than we count the blows, we count the days the weeks the years the centuries the eons until the white laws and commerce and customs will rot in the deserts they've created, lie bleached.

Gloria Anzaldúa, *Borderlands/La Frontera: The New Mestiza* (1987)

En unas pocas centurias [In a few centuries], the future will belong to the *mestiza*. Because the future depends on the breaking down of paradigms, it depends on the straddling of two or more cultures. By creating a new mythos—that is, a change in the way we perceive reality, the way we see ourselves, and the ways we behave—*la mestiza* creates a new consciousness.

Gloria Anzaldúa, *Borderlands/La Frontera: The New Mestiza* (1987)

Don't give in *mi prietita* [my little dark one]
tighten your belt, endure.

Your lineage is ancient,
your roots like those of the mesquite
firmly planted, digging underground
toward that current, the soul of *tierra madre* [mother earth]—
your origin.

Gloria Anzaldúa, *Borderlands/La Frontera: The New Mestiza* (1987)

Leo Araguz (Pharr, Texas, 1970)

One of the smallest players in the National Football League, punter Leo Araguz was turned down by three teams before signing with the Oakland Raiders. This Tejano's ambition is to open a sports camp for kids.

I'd get cut [from a team], and then I'd just work harder.

Latina (October 1998)

I'm happy with myself. That's the way my mama made me.

Latina (October 1998)

Arturo Arias (Guatemala City, Guatemala, 1950)

Cowriter of the screenplay for the popular film *El Norte* (1983), Arturo Arias has published six novels and two books of literary criticism. He is a winner of the Casa de las Américas Award and the Anna Seghers Scholarship for two of his novels. Arias is director of Latin American studies at the University of Redlands, California.

I have always preferred the agony of losing a certain destiny in order to find my true self. Shipwrecked in a hollow, unauthentic world, I prefer to advance staggeringly toward the authenticity of life, even though it might lead me only toward the authenticity of my own death.

Original quotation for this book (July 2001)

I am condemned to live on the border of a death which will not come until I have felt in my body hunger, thirst, cold, warmth, exhaustion, nakedness, pain and illness, and, in my soul, deception, persecution, envy, disdain, dishonor, fear, sadness, ire and desperation, because this is the fate of those, like me, who are condemned to fight for justice until we have built a realm of happiness that will end the prison of calamities imposed by those who, believing they are superior and in possession of the only Truth, have persecuted and enslaved peoples, nations and beliefs that were not forged in their own image.

Original quotation for this book (July 2001)

Desi Arnaz (Santiago, Cuba, 1917–1986)

Born Desiderio Alberto Arnaz y de Acha, Desi Arnaz was a vocalist, drummer, band leader, composer, stage and screen actor, television pro-

Arturo Arias. Photo by Janjaap Dekker. Courtesy of Mr. Arias.

ducer and director. He is best remembered for his role as Ricky Ricardo in the television series *I Love Lucy*, costarring his former wife, comedienne Lucille Ball.

> Once, in Cuba, I was very peeved at my dad for some childish reason and I said to my mother, "Who does he think he is? . . . You always treat him as if he were a king." I will never forget her answer: "That's the only way that I can be a queen."
>
> Desi Arnaz, *A Book* (1976)

> As I stepped down from the ferryboat that brought me from Cuba to the United States of America at Key West, it might not have been a giant step for mankind, but it was a big one for me.
>
> Desi Arnaz, *A Book* (1976)

> The next few lines I used were the oldest in history—and the corniest.
> "Do you know how to rumba, Lucille?"
> "No, I've never learned."
> "Would you like me to teach you how to rumba?"
>
> Desi Arnaz, *A Book* (1976)

A visiting French actor explained his addiction to the show in this manner: "It has the reality of 'l'amour,' or as you say, sex. While it is possible to believe that other husband and wife comedy teams share the same bedroom, it is not possible to believe that they do so with pleasure. Lucy and Ricky skirmish in the daytime so they can 'reconcile' at night."

Desi Arnaz, A Book (1976)

I must admit that I was an old-fashioned Latin, raised observing and believing in the classic double standard. Your wife is your wife and you want to know that you can trust her and be secure in that knowledge. Your fooling around can in no way affect your love for her. That relationship is sacred and a few peccadilloes mean nothing. Lucy knew this.

Desi Arnaz, A Book (1976)

Lucie Arnaz (Los Angeles, California, 1951)

The daughter of Hollywood stars Lucille Ball and Desi Arnaz, Lucie Arnaz has earned a name for herself as an actress on stage and in television and film. She has won the Los Angeles Drama Critics Award for acting.

[On the stage] It's my medium, where I feel most at home, and I love it!

Ladies' Home Journal (October 1990)

María Celeste Arrarás (Mayagüez, Puerto Rico, 1960)

After starting in television in Puerto Rico, María Celeste Arrarás moved to the United States, where she has been a host and newscaster for Univisión in California and Florida. She is also a journalist and author of a book on the late Tejana singer Selena.

I was a swimmer and I learned to see life as a competition, to persevere; and never to give up. I refuse to accept a no. I have a very hard head and a lot of self-confidence.

Cristina (October 2000)

People don't see me as a star . . . but as somebody in the family, because they see me [on television] every day.

Cristina (October 2000)

I am convinced that kindness triples itself in good things.

Cristina (October 2000)

Even though I've gotten many job offers in the Anglo market, I never accepted because I refuse to be hired as the "token Hispanic." I'd rather be the head of the mouse than the tail of the lion! I prefer making a difference in the Latin media to being hired in order to fill a quota on

María Celeste Arrarás. Courtesy of Ms. Arrarás and Univisión.

the English networks. . . . In a decade we'll be the largest minority in the United States, so this mouse is about to roar.

Original quotation for this book (June 2001)

B

Jimmy Santiago Baca (Santa Fe, New Mexico, 1957)

A Mexican American who taught himself to read and write while in prison, Jimmy Santiago Baca has published six books of poetry and a collection of essays. He has also written plays and novels. Baca has won the National Endowment for the Arts Poetry Award, the American Book Award and the Pushcart Prize. He has held the Wallace Stevens Chair at Yale University and the Regents Berkeley Chair at the University of California.

> Carried in my *hefito's* [dad's] arms to the *cantinas* [bars], I would sit on the table and listen to the quarrels of men thinking of selling land, of keeping land, or of having been cheated out of land.
>
> Wolfgang Binder (ed.), *Partial Autobiographies: Interviews with Twenty Chicano Poets* (1985)

Judith F. Baca (Los Angeles, California, 1946)

Founder of the first mural program sponsored by the city of Los Angeles, Judy Baca was artistic director of the famous work "The Great Wall of L.A." This mural was five years in the painting, employed 40 ethnic scholars, 450 young people of various cultural backgrounds, 40 assisting artists and 100 support staff and is a half-mile long. Baca's murals address issues of peace, war, cooperation and spiritual growth.

> [On lowriders, road-hugging customized cars] [Chicanos] took junk and created art. The boulevards were not nice places to be, but once the lowriders started cruising them, they became something else.
>
> *New York Times* (February 19, 2000)

Judith F. Baca. Courtesy of Ms. Baca and the Social and Public Art Resource Center.

I struggle not to be lost from my culture because I think it is the very spirit of how I work. My work is informed by my connection. There's force in the connection. It is the base from which my work flows.

Original quotation for this book (April 2000)

The constant is yourself. And, the extension of yourself is your work.

Original quotation for this book (April 2000)

Alberto V. Báez (Puebla, Mexico, 1912)

During a long career as a physicist, Alberto Báez has taught and conducted research at various universities. He has also worked for UNESCO in New York City and Paris. Báez received the Dennis Gabor Award for his role in X-ray imaging optics. He is the father of singer Joan Báez.

All my early childhood, up to the point where I was going to high school, I feel my entire education was deeply affected by my Mexican upbringing. I realize now that I'm not a Mexican in the typical sense. First, most Mexicans have been brought up in the Catholic environment, and many who come to this country come under different circumstances than I. My own background is preachers [Protestant] and teachers.

Marilyn P. Davis, *Mexican Voices/American Dreams* (1990)

Now when I go back [to Mexico] I don't really go back as a Mexican, but as an internationalist, someone who has been around the world, who realizes that he was born in Mexico, who feels that perhaps there is something special for me to do there. . . . I realize that I don't know enough about the political or economic life. There are whole ranges of Mexican activity that I don't know or comprehend, but I don't think it matters, because when I do go back I find people who are interested in what I can offer and who are saying, yes, come help us. That's a nice feeling.

Marilyn P. Davis, *Mexican Voices/American Dreams* (1990)

We have this image of lazy Mexicans, but I can't imagine a group of Americans doing the stoop labor that the Mexicans do in our fields. That image is obviously wrong. The Mexican is capable of doing hard, hard labor. And when you get the head of Coca-Cola, a Mexican [later president of Mexico Vicente Fox], running a company like that, you know that Mexicans are capable of high-powered business too.

Marilyn P. Davis, *Mexican Voices/American Dreams* (1990)

Joan Báez (Staten Island, New York, 1941)

Born of a father from Mexico and a mother from Scotland, Joan Báez is a famous folk singer in both English and Spanish and a constant advocate for peace and civil rights. With the help of Ira Sandperl, she founded and financed the Institute for the Study of Nonviolence. Báez has several gold singles and eight gold albums, including her hit "Gracias a la vida" (Thanks to Life), sung almost entirely in Spanish.

You don't get to choose how you're going to die. Or when. You can only decide how you're going to live. Now.

Joan Báez, *Daybreak* (1968)

If it's natural to kill, why do men have to go into training to learn how?

Joan Báez, *Daybreak* (1968)

There's a consensus out that it's OK to kill when your government decides who to kill. If you kill inside the country you get in trouble. If you kill outside the country, right time, right season, latest enemy, you get a medal.

Joan Báez, *Daybreak* (1968)

To sing is to love and to affirm, to fly and soar, to coast into the hearts of the people who listen, to tell them that life is to live, that love is there,

Joan Báez. Photo by Wolman. Courtesy of Photofest.

that nothing is a promise, but that beauty exists, and must be hunted for and found. That death is a luxury, better to be romanticized and sung about than dwelt upon in the face of life.

Joan Báez, *Daybreak* (1968)

If we don't sit down and shut up once in a while we'll lose our minds even earlier than we had expected. Noise is an imposition on sanity, and we live in very noisy times.

Joan Báez, *Daybreak* (1968)

I was born gifted. I can speak of my gifts with little or no modesty, but with tremendous gratitude, precisely because they are gifts, and not things which I created, or actions about which I might be proud.

Joan Báez, *And a Voice to Sing With: A Memoir* (1987)

My greatest gift, given to me by forces which confound genetics, environment, race, or ambition, is a singing voice. My second greatest gift, without which I would be an entirely different person with an entirely different story to tell, is a desire to share that voice, and the bounties it has heaped on me, with others.

Joan Báez, *And a Voice to Sing With: A Memoir* (1987)

One of the first problems I had to confront in junior high school was my ethnic background. . . . There I was, with a Mexican name, skin, and hair: the Anglos couldn't accept me because of all three, and the Mexicans couldn't accept me because I didn't speak Spanish.

Joan Báez, *And a Voice to Sing With: A Memoir* (1987)

Through all these changes my social and political views have remained astoundingly steadfast. I have been true to the principles of nonviolence, developing a stronger and stronger aversion to the ideologies of both the far right and the far left and a deeper sense of rage and sorrow over the suffering they continue to produce all over the world.

Joan Báez, *And a Voice to Sing With: A Memoir* (1987)

Antonio Banderas (Málaga, Spain, 1960)

Already well known in Spain and Europe, actor Antonio Banderas became a household name in the United States in the early 1990s. He has performed in more than 40 films. He and his wife, the actress Melanie Griffith, have their own production company, Green Moon.

I remember I couldn't even [afford] to take a bus, so I had to walk six miles to get an audition.

Entertainment Weekly (October 6, 1995)

Working with Melanie Griffith [his wife the actress] is like driving a Ferrari.

People en Español (December 1999/January 2000)

Louis Barajas (Unknown place and date of birth)

At age fifteen, Louis Barajas defended his father in an audit by the Internal Revenue Service. After graduating with a Master's degree in business from Claremont Graduate School, he became a financial planner. His firm in Boyle Heights, Los Angeles, specializes in helping Hispanic clients.

What I'm trying to do in this community is not create change, but transformation.

Lexington Herald-Leader (April 16, 2000)

We forget about what's really significant in our lives . . . helping each other out.

Lexington Herald-Leader (April 16, 2000)

We're constantly looking for somebody to put down, saying things like [boxer] Oscar de la Hoya came from East L.A., he's just like us, he's not special. Instead of saying, "We're all special."

Lexington Herald-Leader (April 16, 2000)

Javier Bardem (Gran Canaria, Spain, 1969)

Since first appearing before a camera at age four, actor Javier Bardem has worked with outstanding directors in Spain and other countries. At the 2001 Oscars he was nominated for Best Actor in *Before Night Falls* (2000).

> In the beginning of my career I had this idea that without suffering there is no art, and that's not true.
>
> *Interview* (January/April 2001)

> The difficult thing is to take your ego and your vanity and throw it in the garbage, and let yourself be taken over by the role. And if you can do that, then you're changed as a human being, because you've seen the world with different eyes.
>
> *Interview* (January/April 2001)

> When you play a character that really exists or existed, the thing that concerns you is respect—for the people who loved this person and are still alive.
>
> *Interview* (January/April 2001)

> I want to act because I don't know how to do anything else. But don't call me an actor. I'm just a worker. I am an entertainer. Don't say that what I am doing is art.
>
> *Guardian Unlimited* (March 21, 2001)

> I'm not crazy about getting rich and famous in Hollywood. I'm already that here in Spain.
>
> *Lexington Herald-Leader* (March 23, 2001)

Rubén Benítez (Chivilcoy, Argentina, 1928)

After studying at the University of Buenos Aires, Rubén Benítez moved to the United States where he began a brilliant academic career as a professor of Spanish literature. During more than thirty years at UCLA, he inspired many students. Benítez is the author of numerous books and articles.

> We don't have to be so proud of our intelligence. Intelligence is a general trait of the human race, as common and natural as the paws of the tiger or the trunk of the elephant. In this age of computers, we are producing machines with "artificial intelligence." Kindness, generosity, compassion, and other moral qualities, which are not present in animals and cannot be reproduced technologically, are human attributes less common and more valuable than intelligence.
>
> Original quotation for this book (January 2001)

In my long career as a university professor, I have always found that the basic personality trait that makes some students more successful than others, in the academy and in the outside world, is the will power and the determination to succeed.

Original quotation for this book (January 2001)

To learn a language different from our own is to open a door to the acceptance of human differences, to tolerance for other ways of thinking and to the understanding, appreciation and love for human values independently of races, languages and social diversities.

Original quotation for this book (January 2001)

Sandra Benítez (Washington, D.C., 1941)

Puerto Rican and Midwestern by heritage, writer Sandra Benítez grew up in Mexico, El Salvador and Missouri. She was the Hispanic Mentor for the Loft Inroads Program from 1989 to 1992. Benítez has received the Minnesota Book Award and a Loft-McKnight Award of Distinction for fiction. She donated part of the royalties from her first novel, *A Place Where the Sea Remembers* (1993), to Nuestros Pequeños Hermanos (Our Little Brothers and Sisters), Cuernavaca, Mexico.

[French writer Gustave] Flaubert said, "Talent is a long patience." The same can be said of fiction writing. Since I began, I have struggled to keep impatience at bay, and now, a mere thirteen years later, my first book is a reality. *Bendito sea* [Thank God].

Acknowledgments, A Place Where the Sea Remembers (1993)

Gracias, mil gracias, Espíritu Santo [Thanks, a thousand thanks, Holy Spirit] for never failing to whisper in my ear.

Acknowledgments, A Place Where the Sea Remembers (1993)

I came to writing late. I was 39 before I gathered enough courage to begin. When I hear other writers talk about writing, or what they have to say about their art, I am amazed by those who say they always knew they had to write.

Contemporary Authors (1994)

Being a writer was something magical I never dreamed I could attain. When I was young, it was a doctor I planned to be. Becoming a doctor seemed much more possible than being a writer. But while growing up, I frequently had a book in my lap and so I was linked, even then, to writing and to the spell that stories cast.

Contemporary Authors (1994)

The heart has four small chambers, but it can hold a world of grief.

Sandra Benítez, Bitter Grounds (1997)

Samuel Betances (New York, New York, 1941)

Although he was born in the continental United States, Samuel Betances was reared in Puerto Rico. A high-school dropout, he went on to earn a doctorate in education from Harvard University. He has been a professor of sociology, partner in a consulting firm, host of a television show and a motivational speaker.

> I've learned to poke fun at myself about issues related to my body, social identity, gender relationship, absurd assumptions and fears, and [about] how I have grown and unlearned bad lessons while learning new good ones.
>
> Matt S. Meier, *Notable Latino Americans* (1997)

Rubén Blades (Panama City, Panama, 1948)

The most famous citizen of his native Panama, Rubén Blades is a composer, singer, band leader, actor and political activist. In addition to gold records presented by recording companies, he has received two Grammy Awards and was the first Hispanic to receive the National Cable Award for acting (ACE).

> We're all looking for America . . . the most dynamic, most diverse and beautiful continent in the world today.
>
> *Américas* (March/April 1984)

> Why cross over to crap? Instead of crossover, I say we should think of convergence.
>
> *Américas* (March/April 1984)

> [My paternal grandmother was a] wonderfully crazy woman who practiced levitation and instilled in me the silly notion that justice is important.
>
> *Time* (July 2, 1984)

> My grandmother was one of the most educated people that I ever met. She was one of the first women to graduate from high school in Panama, when there was no university available. She practiced Yoga, wrote poems and fought for a woman's right to vote.
>
> *Urban Latino*, No. 22 (1999)

> I started in the mailroom . . . , and one day there was a need for a singer in the Ray Barreto Orchestra. Ray heard that I had been singing in Panama when I was younger. He went into the mailroom and auditioned me right there. I passed . . . and that is how I started.
>
> *Urban Latino*, No. 22 (1999)

> [On his candidacy for the presidency of Panama] At no moment did I think I was going to become president, but if I would have, it would

not have been through a desire for power. What we attempted was to bring to the fore the existence of an important sector of the Panamanian population that disagrees and cannot identify with the policies applied to them. My political campaign fully achieved that purpose.

Urban Latino, No. 22 (1999)

I think things are gonna get better. I believe that we are in a process of revolution in terms of democratic institutions. I have tremendous faith in my country.

Urban Latino, No. 22 (1999)

Bobby Bonilla (New York, New York, 1963)

A versatile athlete who has played several positions for the Los Angeles Dodgers, the Pittsburgh Pirates and the New York Mets, Bobby Bonilla attended New York Technical College before entering the major leagues. He was chosen for the National League all-star team for three consecutive years.

Kids today are looking for idols, but sometimes they look too far. . . . They don't have to look any farther than their home because those are the people that love you. They are the real heroes.

USA Today (March 30, 1989)

Henry Bonilla (San Antonio, Texas, 1954)

After a successful career as a television newscaster, in 1992 Henry Bonilla became the first Hispanic Republican elected to the U.S. Congress.

Latinos brought to this country their ethics of hard work and responsibility. During the Depression, my grandfather refused welfare as long as he had a few goats to feed his family. I thank my lucky stars that my forefathers had the vision to come to America and give us all a fair shot.

George (July 1999)

Alicia Borinsky (Buenos Aires, Argentina)

Leaving her native Argentina because of the military dictatorship (1976–83), writer and teacher Alicia Borinsky moved to the United States and studied Hispanic literature. She is a poet, critic and professor at Boston University.

Writing for me is very much a part of my everyday life. I am not the kind of person who thinks of writing as occurring part of the day. Through my daily experiences I have, shall we say, a third eye, that is looking and hearing everything that happens and thinks of recasting it in print.

Joseph M. Palmisano (ed.), *Notable Hispanic American Women*, Book II (1998)

Bárbara Brinson-Pineda (San Francisco, California, 1951)

Bárbara Brinson-Pineda is a poet of Mexican American ancestry.

> Writing is like good sex. It is like you give so much from yourself, and you get so much back, and yet it is like an inspiration. It is like you leave yourself, and yet you are yourself even more.
>
> Wolfgang Binder (ed.), *Partial Autobiographies: Interviews with Twenty Chicano Poets* (1985)

Cruz Bustamante (Dinuba, California, 1958)

When he was elected Lieutenant Governor in 1998, Cruz Bustamante became the first Latino to hold statewide office in California in more than 120 years. A first-generation American, he served as speaker of the state Assembly from 1996 to 1998. President Clinton appointed him to serve on the board that monitored the national census for 2000. Bustamante also sits on the University of California Board of Regents and is a trustee of California State University.

> Our politics have been de-ghettoized. Just because we have exotic last names or darker faces, our politics are assumed to be radical. But that's simply not the case. Ours is very much an American agenda.
>
> *George* (July 1999)

C

Rafael Campo (Dover, New Jersey, 1964)

Rafael Campo teaches and practices medicine at Harvard Medical School and Beth Israel Deaconess Medical Center in Boston. He has developed a method in which his patients read and write poetry as part of the healing process. Dr. Campo is author of *What the Body Told* (1997) and *The Desire to Heal: A Doctor's Education in Empathy, Identity and Poetry* (1998).

> Soul-numbing managed care and mind-boggling technological advancement seem to have conspired to distance doctors from patients. The addition of an increasingly aged and multicultural society creates chasms so wide they threaten to swallow us all. It makes one wonder how anyone can make sense of the experience of illness.
>
> *El Andar* (Spring 2000)

> Creative self-expression has been an important part of healing since the beginning of recorded human history. This ancient truth is being validated today. . . . Patients stricken with asthma or debilitating rheumatoid arthritis actually improved over the course of months just by writing imaginatively about stressful experiences.
>
> *El Andar* (Spring 2000)

> It's not at all that surprising that poetry—whose soothing rhythms have their origins in our physical bodies, in the ebb and flow of our breathing and sobbing, in the very beating of our hearts—can be so effective in restoring empathy and thus kindling the healing process.
>
> *El Andar* (Spring 2000)

> While it would certainly be wrong to say that poetry can cure cancer or AIDS or depression, it is fair to consider how reading and writing poetry

can help those who are "intoxicated" by illness, to borrow from the title of literary critic Anatole Broyard's indelible memoir of his battle with prostate cancer.

El Andar (Spring 2000)

Jorge Campos (Acapulco, Mexico, 1966)

One of Mexico's leading soccer players, Jorge Campos played for his country in the World Cup in 1994 and 1998. He is a versatile athlete who plays both goalie and forward. Campos recently signed with the Chicago Fire to begin his career in major league soccer.

I had a very warm upbringing and I want the same for my family.

Latina (October 1998)

José Canseco (Havana, Cuba, 1964)

One of the most sensational and controversial players of the 1980s and 1990s, José Canseco ranks among the greatest power-hitters in baseball

José Canseco. Courtesy of the National Baseball Hall of Fame Library, Cooperstown, N.Y.

history. He was named Rookie of the Year in 1986 and Player of the Year in 1988 by both the Associated Press and *Sporting News*. Canseco led the Oakland A's to the American League pennant and a World Series victory in 1989.

> I love playing baseball, but sometimes I feel like the gorilla in the zoo. People watch the gorilla, stare at it, trying to figure out why it's doing what it's doing.
>
> *Sports Illustrated* (October 2, 1999)

Mariah Carey (Long Island, New York, 1970)

Daughter of an opera singer and an aerospace engineer, Mariah Carey is known for her seven-octave range and her popular, gospel-influenced, dance-pop songs. She has taken an active role in her career, producing, cowriting and arranging most of her material. Carey has won two Grammy Awards. She has recently embarked on a career in film.

> I think there's something in me that will always remain the little kid who felt like the rug could be pulled out from under her.
>
> *Biography* (February 2000)

> I saw a lot of craziness . . . but I made the right decisions by looking at people who made the wrong decisions, and saying, "I'm not going to be like that."
>
> *Biography* (February 2000)

> I don't think anyone knows as much about what's right for me as I do.
>
> *Biography* (February 2000)

> When I was a little girl, I made a wish that one day I would be singing and writing professionally and doing what I love for a living . . . I never really imagined that it could get to this level.
>
> *Mariah Makes Two Fans' Wishes Come True at the AMA's* Web site (2000)

> I don't get it. I'm a nice, down-to-earth person. There are a lot meaner people in this industry, but somehow everyone had decided I'm the prima donna. Believe me, if I decided I wanted to be a diva, you'd know it. But you're barking up the wrong tree.
>
> *Mariah Makes Two Fans' Wishes Come True at the AMA's* Web site (2000)

Mary Carillo (Queens, New York, 1957)

After four years on the women's professional tennis tour and a mixed-doubles title with her partner John McEnroe at the French Open (1977), Mary Carillo retired from the circuit. She became one of the leading sportscasters in the world. Although she specializes in tennis commentary, Carillo has also covered skiing, women's gymnastics and baseball and two Olympic Games. She has worked for CBS, NBC and HBO.

> [On being called the best female expert on tennis] I don't want to be graded on a curve.
>
> *Sports Illustrated* (June 17, 1991)

Vikki Carr (El Paso, Texas, 1940)

Born Florencia Bisenta de Casillas Martínez Cardona, Vikki Carr is one of the most successful Hispanic recording artists of all time. She has recorded forty-nine albums, seventeen of them golden. In 1985 she won a Grammy for her Spanish-language album *Cosas de Mujer* and repeated in 1992 with *Cosas de Amor,* named the Best Latin Pop Album of the Year. Carr has performed at the White House for several presidents. She is founder of the Vikki Carr Scholarship Foundation, which has helped young Mexican Americans for the past three decades.

> [On the children in the Vikki Carr Scholarship Foundation] I don't have any children of my own, but all of these youngsters are like my own family.
>
> *Saturday Evening Post* (September 1975)

> God knows why He does things. I lost two children, but He has given me much more, and a career to which I am married until death separates us.
>
> *La Opinión* (April 30, 1992)

> For business I'm very American, but my heart is totally Latin.
>
> *La Opinión* (April 30, 1992)

Lynda Carter (Phoenix, Arizona, 1951)

Widely known for her role as television's Wonder Woman in the 1970s, Lynda (Córdoba) Carter began her career as a nightclub singer and dancer. She has starred in various made-for-television movies and in her own variety shows. Carter portrayed the Hollywood legend Rita Hayworth in a controversial TV movie, *The Love Goddess.* She has received many honors, including the Hispanic Woman of the Year Award in 1983.

> [On playing the role of Rita Hayworth] I really wanted the challenge. We both had Hispanic backgrounds. We were both in show business at an early age. We both sing and dance. We were both married to our managers.
>
> *People* (November 7, 1983)

Lourdes Casal (Havana, Cuba, 1938–1981)

Writer and activist Lourdes Casal taught at Rutgers and other universities, publishing extensively in the fields of psychology and the social sciences. She sought to reconcile Cuban exiles with the government of Fidel Castro. Casal helped to found the Instituto de Estudios Cubanos. She won many awards including the Cintas Fellowship from the Institute for International Education.

> I looked in the telephone book, and, sure enough, under the heading of the city government, I found the number of the Commission for the Preservation of Human Resources. I dialed the number, and a syrupy, seductive voice screeched: "This is a recording. The number you have reached has been temporarily disconnected. I repeat this is a recording."
>
> *Los fundadores* (1973)

Pablo Casals (Vendrell, Spain, 1876–1973)

The famous cellist, conductor, composer and humanitarian Pablo Casals vowed never to return to his native Spain as long as the dictator Francisco Franco was in power, and kept his word. He spent his final sixteen years of exile in Puerto Rico, where he initiated the annual Pablo Casals Festival in 1957.

> The cello is like a beautiful woman who has not grown older, but younger with time, more slender, more supple, more graceful.
>
> *Time* (April 29, 1957)

> I am perhaps the oldest musician in the world. I am an old man but in many senses a very young man. And this is what I want you to be, young, young all your life, and to say things to the world that are true.
>
> *Time* (October 23, 1973)

> To retire is the beginning of death.
>
> Peter J. Lawrence, *Peter's Quotations: Ideas for Our Times* (1977)

> [His final words, spoken in an ambulance en route to the hospital] The driver's a maniac! He'll kill us all!
>
> Robert Baldock, *Pablo Casals* (1992)

Rosemary Casals (San Francisco, California, 1948)

The daughter of poor immigrants from El Salvador, tennis star Rosemary Casals won her first championship at the age of thirteen. She was known especially as a superb doubles player, with partners such as Chris Everts Lloyd and Billie Jean King.

I wanted to *be* someone. I knew I was good, and winning tournaments—
it's a kind of way of being accepted.

> Alida M. Thacher, *Raising a Racket: Rosie Casals* (1976)

The other kids had nice tennis clothes, nice rackets, nice white shoes
and came in Cadillacs. I felt stigmatized because we were poor.

> *People* (May 31, 1982)

Carlos Castaneda (Cajamarca, Peru, 1925)

Anthropologist, writer and shaman, Carlos Castaneda is the author of the
controversial, best-selling series of books based on his mentor, Don Juan
Matus, including *The Teachings of Don Juan: A Yaqui Way of Knowledge*
(1968), *A Separate Reality: Further Conversations with Don Juan* (1971) and
Journey to Ixtlan: The Lessons of Don Juan (1972).

> The only thing one can be is an impeccable mediator. One is not the
> player in this cosmic match of chess, one is simply a pawn on the chess-
> board. What decides everything is a conscious impersonal energy that
> sorcerers call *intent* or *the Spirit*.
>
> *Uno Mismo*, Chile (February 1997)

> For thirty years, people have accused Carlos Castaneda of creating a
> literary character simply because what I report to them does not concur
> with the anthropological "a priori," the ideas established in the lecture
> halls or in the anthropological field work.
>
> *Uno Mismo*, Chile (February 1997)

> One needs a lifetime to be able to acquire membership in a cultural
> world. I've been working for more than thirty years in the cognitive
> world of the shamans of ancient Mexico and, sincerely, I don't believe
> I have acquired the membership that would allow me to draw conclu-
> sions or to even propose them.
>
> *Uno Mismo*, Chile (February 1997)

> It is imperative to leave aside what he [Don Juan] called "personal his-
> tory." To get away from the "me" is something extremely annoying and
> difficult. What shamans like Don Juan seek is a state of fluidity where
> the personal "me" does not count.
>
> *Uno Mismo*, Chile (February 1997)

> The goal of Don Juan's shamanism is to break the parameters of his-
> torical and daily perception and to perceive the unknown. That's why
> he called himself a navigator of humanity. He asserted that infinity lies
> beyond the parameters of daily perception. To break these parameters
> was the aim of his life.
>
> *Uno Mismo*, Chile (February 1997)

The pragmatic value of perceiving energy directly as it flows in the universe for a man of the 21st century or a man of the 1st century is the same. It allows him to enlarge the limits of his perception and to use this enhancement within the realm.

Uno Mismo, Chile (February 1997)

Elena Castedo (Barcelona, Spain, 1937)

An acclaimed writer in both Spanish and English, Elena Castedo was born in Spain and raised in Chile. She studied at UCLA and Harvard University. Her novel *Paradise* (1990) was nominated for the National Book Award in the United States and was a best-seller in Spain and Chile.

I'm an immigrant who went through poverty, waited for buses for hours. I bought day old bread. But I don't see myself as part of a Latino literary movement. My interest is human experience and emotions. The immigrant experience is a universal one.

Publishers Weekly (February 1, 1991)

Ana Castillo (Chicago, Illinois, 1953)

A leading figure in the boom of Latina writers in the 1990s, Ana Castillo was educated at Northeastern Illinois University, University of Chicago and the University of Bremen. She is the author of novels, collections of poetry and essays. Her novel *The Mixquiahuala Letters* (1986) won an American Book Award and Before Columbus Foundation Prize; *So Far from God* (1993) won the Carl Sandburg Literary Award in fiction and the Mountains and Plains Booksellers Award; *Peel My Love Like an Onion* (1999) is her best selling novel to date.

The experience of [the Virgin of] Guadalupe is not necessarily a somber one, even if it is always transcendental. There are lighter, extremely personal accounts of Guadalupe's meaning, which may place a frown on the conservative guadalupanos, but we make no claim to represent the Catholic Church here, thank goddess.

Ana Castillo (ed.), *Goddess of the Americas. Diosa de las Américas. Writings on the Virgin of Guadalupe* (1996)

Such dark days in America, long past those of the Great Depression that white America recalls so vividly, still exist. Illness, infant mortality, and all manner of travesty that visit the impoverished are a rolling force today throughout our countryside and cities.

Ana Castillo (ed.), *Goddess of the Americas. Diosa de las Américas. Writings on the Virgin of Guadalupe* (1996)

I remember him dark. Or sometimes I remember *it* darkly. Yes, he was dark.

Peel My Love Like an Onion (1999)

Someone catch me, I'm falling in love. Nothing too serious, no ambulance will be necessary. Just a few days of bed rest is needed, I'm sure. With him.

Peel My Love Like an Onion (1999)

You never feel right saying that—*my country*. For some reason looking Mexican means you can't be American. And my cousins tell me, the ones who've gone to Mexico but were born on this side like me, that over there they're definitely not Mexican.

Peel My Love Like an Onion (1999)

Lauro F. Cavazos (King Ranch, Texas, 1927)

When he was sworn in as U.S. Secretary of Education in 1988, Lauro F. Cavazos became the first Hispanic American cabinet officer in the country's history. He earned a doctorate in anatomy, taught at several universities and served as president of his alma mater, Texas Tech University.

[My goal is to] reawaken in every child in this country the thirst, the cry, the hunger for education.

Charles Moritz (ed.), *Current Biography Yearbook* (1989)

You are dealing with a young child, with a person who arrives at school the first day and doesn't understand what's going on, scared to death—scared to death if you can speak English, but it's double when you can't speak English.

Charles Moritz (ed.), *Current Biography Yearbook* (1989)

It is our expectation that the term "dropout" will become obsolete.

Charles Moritz (ed.), *Current Biography Yearbook* (1989)

Orlando Cepeda (Ponce, Puerto Rico, 1937)

Known affectionately as "The Baby Bull" and "Cha-Cha," Orlando Cepeda was a star first baseman for several teams in the National and American Leagues. He was elected to the Baseball Hall of Fame in 1999, the first Puerto Rican to achieve that honor since Roberto Clemente.

I'm a very lucky person to be born with the skills to play baseball. Through baseball, I escaped poverty in Puerto Rico. Through baseball, I built a name for myself. Through baseball, I opened the gate for more Puerto Ricans to come to this country to play baseball for a living.

Kansas City Star (July 24, 1999)

Orlando Cepeda. Courtesy of Photofile.

Hitting [pitcher] Nolan Ryan is like eating soup with a fork.

Kansas City Star (July 24, 1999)

It was meaningful [for me to join other Latin stars in the Baseball Hall of Fame]. Joining my dear friend and brother, Juan Marichal, from the Dominican. Joining Luis Aparicio, from Venezuela, and Rod Carew, from Panama.

Kansas City Star (July 24, 1999)

Lorna Dee Cervantes (San Francisco, California, 1954)

Of Mexican and Native American (Tarascan and Chumash) ancestry, Lorna Dee Cervantes was educated at San Jose State University and the University of California, Santa Cruz. She is a writer and the founder of Mango Publications in San Jose, California. Winner of a grant from the National Endowment for the Arts, Cervantes is the author of several volumes of poetry.

Death can be a friend, death can be an ally, if you accept it.

Wolfgang Binder (ed.), *Partial Autobiographies: Interviews with Twenty Chicano Poets* (1985)

Rafael Chacón (Santa Fe, New Mexico, 1833–1925)

A witness to the end of the Mexican period in the Southwest, Rafael Chacón participated in the commercial, military and political events of early New Mexico. His writings represent one of the few surviving documents of the New Mexican Hispanic point of view. In his seventies, Chacón wrote his memoirs to record for his family the drama, adventure and sorrow of his life.

I am poor and my only inheritance is my honor.

Rafael Chacón Web site (2000)

Franklin Chang-Díaz (San José, Costa Rica, 1950)

After receiving his doctorate in applied physics from the Massachusetts Institute of Technology, Franklin Chang-Díaz became an astronaut with NASA and made numerous space flights. In 1987 he received the Medal of Excellence from the Hispanic Caucus of the U.S. Congress. Chang-Díaz has been a visiting scientist at his alma mater, where he worked on plasma physics for future missions to Mars. In 1993 he was appointed director of the Advanced Space Propulsion Laboratory at the Johnson Space Center.

I came to the United States because I wanted to be an astronaut. . . . It's been my dream since I was seven years old.

Daily Princetonian (May 12, 2000)

I came in 1968 from Costa Rica after finishing high school. I hardly knew any English, but I made it up to Hartford, Connecticut, and convinced the principal to let me enroll in high school there.

Daily Princetonian (May 12, 2000)

Being an astronaut has been every bit what I dreamed it would be. . . . There is nothing more fun than what I do. The view of Earth from the orbiting shuttle is the most amazing thing imaginable!

Daily Princetonian (May 12, 2000)

I have achieved my ultimate dream—to fly in space. That will always be the most important thing to me.

Daily Princetonian (May 12, 2000)

Charo (María Rosario Pilar Martínez) (Murcia, Spain, 1951)

Dancer, singer, composer and comedienne, Charo became a household name with her big blonde hair, shapely figure, flashy clothes, fractured English and the hip-shake she calls the "cuchi-cuchi." She has been named Outstanding Entertainer of the Year by Nosotros, the Hispanic arts organization.

What I do is from the heart. This is what I was born for.

Charo Web site (February 2000)

Spanish is a very poetic and passionate language.

Charo Web site (February 2000)

I love show business, but family is my priority.

Charo Web site (February 2000)

I tell you, I still don't know what the hell "cuchi-cuchi" means. But hey, it works for me!

Charo Web site (February 2000)

Sometimes I think, taking the hours I give to the guitar, when I die, half of my life will have been given to that instrument.

Charo Web site (February 2000)

César Chávez (Yuma, Arizona, 1927–1993)

The son of migrant laborers from Mexico, César Chávez was a union organizer and social activist who founded the National Farm Workers Association (NFWA) and later the United Farm Workers (UFW). For five years he led a boycott against California grape growers, protesting against poor working conditions. The boycott was finally successful in winning new rights for farm workers. In 1994 Chávez was posthumously awarded the Presidential Medal of Freedom, the nation's highest civilian honor.

¡Viva la causa! [Long live the cause!]

César Chávez and His Legacy Web site (UCLA) (1996)

¡Sí se puede! [Yes it can be done!]

César Chávez and His Legacy Web site (UCLA) (1996)

I am convinced that the truest act of courage, the strongest act of manliness is to sacrifice ourselves for others in a totally non-violent struggle for justice.

César Chávez and His Legacy Web site (UCLA) (1996)

If you really want to make a friend, go to someone's house and eat with him. . . . The people who give you their food give you their heart.

César Chávez and His Legacy Web site (UCLA) (1996)

We need to help students and parents cherish and preserve the ethnic and cultural diversity that nourishes and strengthens this community— and this nation.

César Chávez and His Legacy Web site (UCLA) (1996)

César Chávez. Courtesy of Arte Público Press Photo Archives.

A word as to the education of the heart. We don't believe that this can be imparted through books; it can only be imparted through the loving touch of the teacher.

César Chávez and His Legacy Web site (UCLA) (1996)

The end of all education should surely be service to others. We cannot seek achievement for ourselves and forget about the progress and prosperity of our community. Our ambitions must be broad enough to include the aspirations and needs of others for their sake and for our own.

Edward James Olmos, Lea Ybarra and Manuel Monterrey, *Americanos: Latino Life in the United States* (1999)

Denise Chávez (Las Cruces, New Mexico, 1948)

Author of *The Last of the Menu Girls* (1985 Puerto del Sol Fiction Award), *Face of an Angel* (1995 American Book Award) and the one-person show

Denise Chávez. © Cynthia Farah, 1988. Courtesy of the Center for Southwest Research, General Library, University of New Mexico.

Women in the State of Grace, Denise Chávez is artistic director for the Border Book Festival and has taught at New Mexico State University in Las Cruces. She won a Lila Wallace–Reader's Digest Fund Writer's Award for 2000.

> My work is rooted in the Southwest, in heat and dust, and reflects a world where love is as real as the land. In this dry and seemingly harsh and empty world there is much beauty to be found. That hope of the heart is what feeds me, my characters.
>
> *Contemporary Authors New Revision Series* (1991)

Writing for me is a healing, therapeutic, invigorating, sensuous manifestation of the energy that comes to you from the world, from everything that's alive.

Publisher's Weekly (August 15, 1994)

Everything has a voice and you just have to listen as closely as you can. That's what's so exciting—a character comes to you and you can't write fast enough because the character is speaking through you. It's a divine moment.

Publisher's Weekly (August 15, 1994)

I feel, as a Chicana writer, that I am capturing the voice of so many who have been voiceless for years. I write about the neighborhood handymen, the waitresses, the bag ladies, the elevator operators. They all have something in common: they know what it is to love and to be merciful.

Contemporary Authors New Revision Series (1997)

Dennis Chávez (Albuquerque, New Mexico, 1962–1988)

After earning a law degree from Georgetown University and holding several political offices in New Mexico, Dennis Chávez became the first Hispanic to be elected to the U.S. Senate (Democrat). There he fought tirelessly to support education and civil rights. Chávez served five terms in the Senate.

Wherever the common law, unmodified by statute, exists, there injustice exists.

Current Biography (1946)

Linda Chávez (Albuquerque, New Mexico, 1947)

Political commentator, educator and author, Linda Chávez has had a controversial career on many fronts. She was the highest-ranking woman in the Reagan White House and is founder and president of the Center for Equal Opportunity. She was nominated to be Secretary of Labor by President George W. Bush but withdrew her nomination.

I have had more difficulty with what I consider discriminatory and prejudiced behavior from liberals who thought they were doing me a favor than I have ever experienced from bigots.

Washington Post (January 30, 1984)

I really love this country and what it stands for, and the way in which it allows people like me to make it on their own, on their own initiative and hard work.

Washington Post (January 30, 1984)

Dennis Chávez. Courtesy of the Center for Southwest Research, General Library, University of New Mexico.

I think I still have that sense that if you work hard enough, you'll make it, and I don't think it does a service to people when you say, "Well, you don't have to work very hard because we'll give you a preference."

Washington Post (January 30, 1984)

I made it on hard work.

Washington Monthly (June 1985)

I guess I'm just stubborn. I do go against the grain. I do things that are not always popular. There's a tenacity there. I guess I've always thought of myself as different and sometimes I've gotten more attention for myself than I wanted.

Christian Science Monitor (December 11, 1986)

I don't speak for anyone but Linda Chávez.

New York Times (August 19, 1998)

We will be the "majority minority" population in the next century. But many forget that a number of those Latinos will themselves be the product of intermarriage with Anglos. Far more Americans will count at least one grandparent of Latino descent by the mid-twenty-first century.

George (July 1999)

[About her father] As a house painter, he taught me the dignity of manual labor. As someone whose own childhood poverty cut short his education in the ninth grade, he nonetheless introduced me to the world of books and ideas. And those are what enabled me to take a path that was easier than his own.

New York Times (January 3, 2001)

My mother . . . stood on her feet long hours in restaurants and in department stores to help support our family during my childhood. . . . [Her] love continues to give me courage.

New York Times (January 3, 2001)

Linda Chávez-Thompson (Lubbock, Texas, 1944)

The daughter of sharecroppers, Linda Chávez-Thompson became the first person of color on the AFL-CIO's executive board. When she was named executive vice-president of the organization, she became the highest-ranking woman in organized labor.

I've walked, talked and done everything a labor leader needed to do to protect her workers.

Business Week (November 13, 1995)

In the past, some people used to suggest that there was one struggle of the union movement for economic progress . . . and a separate struggle of the people with disabilities, people of color, women, immigrants, and lesbians and gays for dignity. But the truth is they are not separate. They are one struggle and one dream.

Current Biography (March 2000)

Henry Cisneros (San Antonio, Texas, 1947)

Educated at Texas A & M, Harvard University and George Washington University, Henry Cisneros was mayor of San Antonio, Secretary of Housing and Urban Development in the Clinton cabinet (1993–97) and President of Univisión Communications. Once considered Hispanics' best hope for national political prominence, in 1999 he admitted to perjury in his confirmation process as Secretary of Housing and Urban Development, paid a $10,000 fine and was not jailed.

[Our cities are] piles of dry wood with red-hot coals underneath.

U.S. News & World Report (April 19, 1993)

We have to be honest, we have to be truthful and speak to the one dirty secret in American life, and that is racism.

U.S. News & World Report (April 19, 1993)

Roberto Clemente (Carolina, Puerto Rico, 1934–1972)

One of the greatest baseball players of all time, the first Hispanic to be elected to the Hall of Fame and a national hero in Puerto Rico, Roberto Clemente led the Pittsburgh Pirates for eighteen seasons until his death

Roberto Clemente. Photo by Luis Ramos. Courtesy of the National Baseball Hall of Fame Library, Cooperstown, N.Y.

in an airplane accident on December 31, 1972, when he was flying relief supplies to victims of an earthquake in Nicaragua.

> [When his friends protested that the aircraft was unsafe, Clemente said before he boarded the plane] If you're going to die, you're going to die.
>
> C. Bernard Ruffin, *Last Words* (1995)

Judith Ortiz Cofer (Hormigueros, Puerto Rico, 1952)

Poet, essayist and fiction writer Judith Ortiz Cofer moved to the United States at a young age. She has taught English at various universities. Cofer has won a fellowship from the National Endowment for the Arts and the Pushcart Prize for nonfiction. Her works include the autobiographical essays *Silent Dancing: A Remembrance of a Puerto Rican Childhood* (1990) and *Latin Deli: Prose and Poetry* (1993).

> It was a challenge, not only to learn English, but to master it enough to teach it and—the ultimate goal—to write poetry in it.
>
> *Contemporary Authors* (1991)

> My family is one of the main topics of my poetry. In tracing their lives, I discover more about mine.
>
> *Contemporary Authors* (1991)

Maria Antonieta Collins (Mexico)

Born and raised in Mexico, Maria Antonieta Collins has lived in the United States since the 1970s. She is a news correspondent and television anchor for Univisión in Miami. Collins has won two Emmy Awards for her reporting.

> The American dream is myself. I'm like a thousand immigrants that come to the United States, with a bag filled with dreams.
>
> Joseph M. Palmisano (ed.), *Notable Hispanic American Women*, Book II (1998)

> Thank you for helping to keep Spanish from dying.
>
> Original quotation for this book (July 2001)

Miriam Colón (Ponce, Puerto Rico, 1945)

As the first lady of Hispanic theater in New York, Miriam Colón founded and directed the Puerto Rican Traveling Theater and cofounded the Círculo Dramático. She has also performed in films and on television. Colón is the recipient of the 1990 White House Hispanic Heritage Award.

> My mother has been the major force in my life. To this day, I am very, very attached to her. She is my role model . . . [and] a wonderful, warm

María Antonieta Collins. Courtesy of Ms. Collins and Univisión.

woman. I am totally sure of her love—the only thing I'm sure of in my life.

Diane Telgen and Jim Kamp (eds.), *Notable Hispanic American Women* (1993)

France Anne Córdova (Paris, France, 1947)

Born in Paris, where her father was stationed with Christian Action Research and Education (CARE), France Anne Córdova grew up in California and studied at Stanford University and California Institute of Technology. After a career as a journalist, she became an astrophysicist with the Los Alamos National Laboratory and NASA. Córdova has also been a university professor, department head, vice-president and vice chancellor of research.

I'm by nature optimistic. Reaching goals isn't for pessimistic people. At all steps of my career, there was someone saying, "I wouldn't do that.

You're too old, too young, too inexperienced." There are always nay-sayers. Ask yourself: What is important to me? What is my vision?
Hispanic Outlook in Higher Education (October 11, 1996)

What's fascinating about science is all the mystery. Who are we? Where did we come from? We are not all there is.
Woman, Santa Barbara News-Press Magazine (Summer 1997)

Ángel Corella (Madrid, Spain, 1975)

After years of dancing in obscurity, Ángel Corella burst onto the scene by winning the Concours International de Dance de Paris. He has performed many leading roles for the American Ballet Theater in New York and is considered one of the greatest dancers in the world.

[Dancing] is like being in love for the first time, and being loved back.
Dance (November 1995)

I'm thinking of every day I had to get up at seven in the morning and go two hours to class. And I feel in this moment I am receiving the reward.
Dance (November 1995)

When I dance, I feel as if I am being moved by something outside myself. It is the feeling of being a puppet.
Dance (November 1995)

When you want something very badly and you don't have it, you forget about it, and then it comes to you. That always happens to me.
Dance (November 1995)

Sometimes I feel like it's sad to say this, but dance is my life. I don't think I could live without dance. I express myself dancing. That's just the way I am.
Stagebill Web site (1999)

I wish everybody could dance. When you worry about something or there's something you don't like, you dance and everything goes away. It's a way to explode.
Stagebill Web site (1999)

Lucha Corpi (Jaltipán, Mexico, 1945)

Poet Lucha Corpi moved to the United States from Mexico when she was seventeen. She writes poetry in both Spanish and English.

It is a sin when you see injustice to keep quiet.
Wolfgang Binder (ed.), *Partial Autobiographies: Interviews with Twenty Chicano Poets* (1985)

Manuel Cortés Castañeda (Rivera, Huila, Colombia, 1956)

A professor of Spanish language and Hispanic literatures in the United States, Manuel Cortés Castañeda has published several volumes of poetry.

> Excessive belief in one's work and blind faith in one's native tongue combine to form the deadly trap that the writer sets for himself to avoid facing the solitude essential to creativity.
>
> *anq (American Notes & Queries)* (Spring 1997)

> Our fears are aroused when we realize that a society supposedly based on the cult of individuality and creativity uses language to reaffirm precisely the opposite.
>
> *anq (American Notes & Queries)* (Spring 1997)

> My greatest concern arises out of the tendency of American society to pretend that everyone is the same and from the fact that it uses language as the fundamental vehicle of this pretense. It sells us the illusion (the American Dream) that even what is impossible is possible, and so we forget that overestimating one's worth leads us down a dead-end street.
>
> *anq (American Notes & Queries)* (Spring 1997)

> They come to this country driven by vulnerability and dreams which remain intact in spite of continual lapses and relapses. Some call them "Latinos." For others they are all "Mexicans" camouflaged in the shadow of a shadow which terrifies us: our own shadow. The prelude to their stay is a clouded mirror transfigured by nostalgia. Then they stay forever though they are not really here and they criticize everything though they partake of everything. In time, without any particular desire to do so they become citizens for no particular reason and the dream, still struggling to keep afloat, returns alone to its place of origin.
>
> Original quotation for this book, translated by Janet Dawn Foley (January 2001)

> What terrifies me the most about people in American society is how out of touch they are with their own bodies, and as a consequence how out of touch they are with the body of another person who is equally out of touch. As for me, it doesn't matter because I've learned to have a little something up my sleeve that I can pull out whenever necessary. Fear comes alive when the neighbor children, horrified, cover their eyes and are seized by a sudden tremor (or an unaccustomed pallor) when, by accident, they see my five-year-old daughter naked or only partially clothed. It is as if at twilight a bird that has long been imprisoned in its cage were to die of a sudden attack.
>
> Original quotation for this book, translated by Janet Dawn Foley (January 2001)

We can certainly say, with no danger of being mistaken, that the American family exists in Hollywood films and in television commercials. It's a product of doubtful quality that has not been able to make a name for itself in the market. It's both comical and pathetic to see how politicians go to great lengths to buy a family that they don't have in the vain hope of feeding a dream that has no substance and no dreamer. Then comes the traditional family portrait and that amorphous construct that they call history. The Latino family so glorified in the tangle of Catholic dogma and unwilling to face up to its own disfigured or transfigured face is not so different from the American portrait. Sadly, we also cling to an image even after the mirror is shattered although we remain longer in the childhood home. It goes without saying that we don't worry about outstanding bills and the market share.

> Original quotation for this book, translated by Janet Dawn Foley (January 2001)

Luigi Crespo (Peru, 1973)

The executive director of the Republican National Hispanic Assembly, Luigi Crespo aims to bring more Latinos into his party.

Our Hispanic ideals are very conservative.

> *Newsweek* Web site (2000)

Celia Cruz (Havana, Cuba, 1924)

With her famous band, La Sonora Matancera, and her signature "¡Azúcar!" (Sugar!), Celia Cruz has performed and recorded many hits over fifty years. "The Queen of Salsa" has received more than 100 awards and honors, including the Hispanic Heritage Lifetime Achievement Award, the Hispanic Women Achievers Award, the Smithsonian Institution's Lifetime Achievement Award, one Grammy and ten Grammy nominations.

Music is what gave me the courage to fight and get out of poverty and touch the universe. . . . The only important thing is music.

> *Más* (November 1991)

I have always felt the same way about music, very deep. Every time I come on stage, I feel like it's the first time that I've sung.

> *New York Times* (January 20, 1997)

It comes natural for me, because it's the same music I've been doing since the beginning. It just has a different name now.

> *New York Times* (January 20, 1997)

Celia Cruz. Courtesy of Photofest.

There is something in me that even I applaud and it is my profession-
alism. I don't mean being a perfectionist but anything I get involved in
I want to do well.

Interview with Juan Esteban, *LaMusica* Web site (1998)

Many reporters ask me to give advice to my fans about love and relationship and I always stress the same thing, communication. People
must talk about the things they did and how they feel about it. . . . It is
good to be an open book, because when you start hiding things from
each other then you start feeling uncomfortable and insecure to the point
in which anger takes over and hurts the couple's relationship.

Interview with Juan Esteban, *LaMusica* Web site (1998)

Just to know that I am helping somebody in a justified struggle makes
me feel happy.

Interview with Juan Esteban, *LaMusica* Web site (1998)

These are exciting times for young Latinos. They are increasingly exposed both to their ancestors' culture and values and to those of the United States. It makes for quite a cocktail, a great pick and choose. My hope is that their generation will choose the best from both worlds.

George (July 1999)

Music is a gift that was given to me by God; unless he takes it away, I will continue to share my gift with the world.

Honorary degree announcement posted by the University of Miami (1999)

Humberto Cruz (Havana, Cuba, 1945)

A native of Cuba whose family came to the United States with only $300 in their pockets, Humberto Cruz studied at the University of Miami. He

Humberto Cruz. © Tribune Media Services, Inc. All rights reserved. Reprinted with permission.

became editor of the Miami-based publication *¡Exito!* and is now the personal finance writer for the Fort Lauderdale–based *Sun-Sentinel* and a syndicated columnist nationwide. His column, "The Savings Game," has run since 1991.

> I'm afraid too many women still rely too much on the men to "take care of the finances," and too many men fail to include the women in financial and investment decisions.
>
> *Lexington Herald-Leader* (December 12, 1999)

> The Y2K non-event proved again that the American people cannot be manipulated that easily. They wisely ignored the incessant coverage and scare headlines.
>
> *Lexington Herald-Leader* (January 30, 2000)

Penélope Cruz (Madrid, Spain, 1974)

The Spanish actress Penélope Cruz (Sánchez) is known for her frequent appearances in the films of her countryman Pedro Almodóvar, notably *Todo sobre mi madre* (All About My Mother), which won the Oscar for the Best Foreign Film (1999). Some of her other movie credits include *Belle Époque* (1992) and *All the Pretty Horses* (2000).

> Acting is like a desperate desire for communication of feelings and emotions. Really, you cannot help it. It's in there, and there's nothing else you want to do. It's like *What is this, this monster that wants to come out?*
>
> *GQ* (February 2000)

> Yes, I feel lost. It's good. You can get to something new when you feel so lost.
>
> *GQ* (February 2000)

> It would be terrible to be secure all the time.
>
> *GQ* (February 2000)

> Sanity and acting and life [are] all about paying attention, being in the moment and seeing what you have in front of you.
>
> *GQ* (February 2000)

> My wish is to keep learning, to keep working. I would like to combine work here [United States] and [in] Spain.
>
> *Movie Talk: Celebrity Interviews* Web site (March 2000)

> I can be very wild.
>
> *Elle* (July 2000)

> I dream in English. . . . But when I want to have fun, I laugh all night in Spanish.
>
> *Elle* (July 2000)

I'm not much of a cook. . . . Right now when dealing with food, I seem to do best at calling room service.

Lexington Herald-Leader (September 24, 2000)

Drugs in my life? Forget it!

Vogue (March 2001)

I don't have a problem about growing older. Many women are proud of every year. I don't like that thing to lie about the age.

Vogue (March 2001)

[On her accent] I think maybe it wouldn't be very smart to lose it completely.

Vogue (March 2001)

Ted Cruz (1971)

The first Latino to clerk for the chief justice of the United States, Ted Cruz is the son of a Cuban immigrant to the United States in 1957.

It would be wonderful if there were more minorities who were working at the court. . . . Typically the court is hiring from those students at the top law schools in the country and for whatever reason, there are very few minorities there. That strikes me as a problem less with the court than with the educational system we have throughout our country.

The News Hour with Jim Lehrer (July 23, 1998)

Education opened the American dream to him [my father]. We're failing to provide that education now, especially to poor minorities.

Newsweek Web site (2000)

Linda García Cubero (Shreveport, Louisiana, 1958)

The daughter of a mother who was an airman second class and a father who was a pilot, Linda García Cubero went on to become the first Hispanic woman to graduate from the Air Force Academy and any of the three service academies. After seven years in the military, she began a successful career in the aerospace industry.

[On her mother who raised five children almost alone] She did it all with love and joy and never showed the pain.

New York Times Magazine (May 5, 1985)

Blanquita Cullum (Ventura, California)

Talk-show host Blanquita Cullum has worked on both radio and television. She served on the Virginia Commission for the Arts and was awarded the Corporate Achievement Award by *Vista* magazine for helping Hispanic Americans enter the broadcasting field.

> When I began there were no Latina role models. I had to cut through the obstacles with a machete of my own.
>
> Joseph M. Palmisano (ed.), *Notable Hispanic American Women*, Book II (1998)

Verónica Cunningham (San Diego, California, 1952)

Like some Chicana poets, Verónica Cunningham does not speak Spanish and writes only in English.

> I have an incredible relationship with the pencil and . . . paper. It's like having a lover that's just pulling out certain truths from inside who you are, putting them out on the table.
>
> Wolfgang Binder (ed.), *Partial Autobiographies: Interviews with Twenty Chicano Poets* (1985)

Roberto Cutie (Unknown place and date of birth)

Chosen from hundreds of priests to host the television program *Padre Alberto* on Telemundo, with its debut in 1999, Roberto Cutie has quickly become a celebrity among the Spanish-speaking population of the United States.

> In life one thing I've learned is you have to learn to laugh at yourself. I crack jokes about myself, for example, because it's laughing a little bit at life itself.
>
> *Estilo* (December 1999)

> Our program is not a preachy show. It's not a religious forum. It's a program about humanity.
>
> *Estilo* (December 1999)

> The best thing I can do is challenge my viewers to help make this a better world and to discover more about themselves no matter what their faith or beliefs are.
>
> *Estilo* (December 1999)

D

Julia de Burgos (San Juan, Puerto Rico, 1914–1953)

One of the greatest poets of Puerto Rico, Julia de Burgos is remembered for her commanding presence and her sharp intellect in addition to her writings. She spent the last eleven years of her life in New York.

> I hunger for freedom. If I die, I do not want this tragic country [the United States] to swallow my bones. They need the warmth of Borinquén [Puerto Rico]. At least let them strengthen the worms there and not here.
>
> Matt S. Meier, *Notable Latino Americans* (1997)

Óscar de la Hoya (Los Angeles, California, 1973)

A gold medalist at the 1992 Olympics, Óscar de la Hoya has been lightweight champion of the World Boxing Organization and the International Boxing Federation, as well as lightweight and welterweight champion of the World Boxing Council. The son of Mexican immigrants, he grew up in East Los Angeles.

> I've been asked to join gangs, but I've never wanted to.
>
> *Sports Illustrated* (October 21, 1991)

> There are fighters . . . who don't get hit. We don't look like fighters. The typical Latino boxing fan doesn't like it.
>
> *Washington Post* (June 6, 1996)

> I won the gold [medal] for my mom. Now the championship will be for me.
>
> Elizabeth A. Schick (ed.), *Current Biography Yearbook* (1997)

I don't follow boxing, and I never did.

GQ (November 1999)

The die-hard boxing fan is ignorant.

GQ (November 1999)

Ángela de Hoyos (Coahuila, Mexico, 1940)

At an early age Ángela de Hoyos moved to San Antonio, Texas, with her family. She is a poet, editor, publisher and freelance visual artist.

I rather like the U.S.A. Where else can you raise so much hell without being put behind bars?

Wolfgang Binder (ed.), *Partial Autobiographies: Interviews with Twenty Chicano Poets* (1985)

Óscar de la Renta (Santo Domingo, Dominican Republic, 1932)

After being educated in his native country, fashion designer Óscar de la Renta moved to the United States and worked for several companies until he founded his own house in 1973. He won the Jack Dempsey Award for humanitarianism in 1998 and the Lifetime Achievement Award of the Fashion Designers of America in 1990.

When I'm recognized by someone from Latin America, they will come up to me and say, "Mr. de la Renta, we are so proud of you." They say this because I am one of theirs; I am a Latino. You'd never have an Italian say to a Frenchman "I am so very proud that you are a European." But that's our great strength: We all feel so close to one another.

George (July 1999)

Dolores del Río (Durango, Mexico, 1905–1983)

A star in silent films and talkies, Lolita Dolores Asúnsolo y López Negrete (del Río) made movies in both her native Mexico and in Hollywood. She founded Estancia Infantil, a day-care center for children of Mexican entertainers.

[On her Estancia Infantil] Babies are special in Mexico, you know, and their first six years are the most important. We play Brahms and Bach to them, teach them English, folklorico dancing—all the arts.

Modern Maturity (February 1981)

Cameron Díaz (San Diego, California, 1973)

After an early career as a model, Cameron Díaz has become one of the most popular actresses in Hollywood, specializing in comic roles in films such as *My Best Friend's Wedding* (1997) and *There's Something about Mary*

(1998). She has won a New York Critics Circle Award for best actress and an American Comedy Award.

> Knowing that you have a support system—family, whatever—really helps. Then you don't need other people's acceptance.
>
> *Interview* (August 1994)

> It's my responsibility to figure out what I want to do. I don't want to play a babe in every movie.
>
> *Sassy* (August 1996)

Junot Díaz (Dominican Republic, 1970)

Drown (1993), the critically acclaimed collection of short stories about his childhood in the Dominican Republic and New Jersey, established Junot Díaz as a new voice of "Generation Ñ." A Guggenheim fellow and winner of a Lila Wallace–Reader's Digest Fund Writer's Award, he teaches cre-

Junot Díaz, author of *Drown*. Photo by Marion Ettlinger.

ative writing at Syracuse University. Díaz is a member of Dominican 2000, a community organization based in New York City.

> There's about fifty books whose very existence make me happy every day to be alive.
>
> *Black Issues Book Review* (March 2001)

> Books were an easy language for me to control. Because when you read something you don't have to pronounce it correctly, you just have to know what it means. . . . And so reading . . . was a place where I could show mastery because speaking was so awful.
>
> *Gráfica* Web site (September 2001)

> In one form or another the Dominican Republic—that world which was almost but not entirely lost—has always haunted me. . . . There were always . . . just over my shoulder, trumpets from the island of my eviction.
>
> New York State Writers Institute Web site (September 2001)

Plácido Domingo (Madrid, Spain, 1941)

The enormous repertoire of the famous tenor Plácido Domingo includes some ninety operas, many of which he knows well enough to perform on sight. Born in Spain, raised in Mexico, he has performed in all of the world's best opera houses. *Three Tenors*, his concert recording with José Carreras and Luciano Pavarotti, has sold more than ten million copies.

> You carry the load for which you have the shoulders.
>
> *Time* (September 27, 1993)

> I always say that my parents not only gave life to me but my career as well: music. I started listening to them, living in their world, this marvelous world that is music and that made them so happy.
>
> *El Universal* (January 11, 2000)

> When I got to know my [future] wife, I remember I serenaded her at night. . . . As it was not a house but an apartment in a three-story building, the police sometimes came and, as they knew me already, said: "Plácido, do hurry up, your neighbors have been calling us."
>
> *El Universal* (January 11, 2000)

> Money is also welcome because it enables you on many occasions to help other people. But any ostentatious display is something I don't like.
>
> *El Universal* (January 11, 2000)

> I cannot bear enviousness. I am happy about the success of others and I do not see it with envy but with satisfaction.
>
> *El Universal* (January 11, 2000)

Like everybody else I hold death in great respect, because anybody who says otherwise is a dreamer or a religious fanatic.

El Universal (January 11, 2000)

John Dos Passos (Chicago, Illinois, 1896–1970)

Son of a Portuguese father, John Dos Passos became one of the most important novelists in the United States, writing works such as *Manhattan Transfer* (1925), *The 42nd Parallel 1919* (1930), *The Big Money* (1936) and *Adventures of a Young Man* (1939). He always showed a special interest in the Hispanic world, as seen in his book *Rosinante to the Road Again* (1922).

I'd like to annihilate these stupid colleges of ours, and all the nice young men therein, instillers of stodginess—every form of bastard culture, middle class snobbism.

Ca. 1912, Richard Hofstadter, *Anti-Intellectualism in American Life* (1963)

People don't choose their careers; they are engulfed by them.

New York Times (October 25, 1959)

[His final words, spoken to his wife] I think I'd like to read the paper now.

C. Bernard Ruffin, *Last Words* (1995)

E

Héctor Elizondo (New York, New York, 1936)

One of the best-known Hispanic actors in the United States, Héctor Elizondo has performed in many plays, films and television programs. He studied at City College of New York and the Ballet Arts Company of Carnegie Hall. Elizondo has won the Lifetime Achievement Image Award, the Obie and the ALMA Award for best actor and the Emmy for best supporting actor. Some of his movie credits include *The Flamingo Kid* (1984), *Pretty Woman* (1990) and *Runaway Bride* (1999).

> I have also been stubborn in refusing to do certain types of roles that feed into that distortion, that feed into that horrible misrepresentation [of Latinos]—the drug dealer of the month, that kind of garbage. I don't know if I wouldn't have done those roles if I had been starving, but it never quite came to it.
>
> *Los Angeles Times* (February 9, 1993)

> Stop calling me a Latino actor until you start calling Al Pacino an Italian actor.
>
> *Latin Style* (September 1999)

> We're going to have to come up with the stories and own the projects. We're not incorporated into the mainstream consciousness. I've often turned down Latino roles because they're written so badly. I didn't come from a family of drug dealers. How come they want me to play drug dealers? Where are the cops, doctors, lawyers, teachers, and bus drivers, the people that really make things happen?
>
> *Latin Style* (September 1999)

> I've always just worked and never denied my culture. In fact I've been pretty outspoken about it.
>
> *Urban Latino*, No. 22 (1999)

Spics are in! Now it's fashionable to be Latino.

Urban Latino, No. 22 (1999)

I'm not going to be a Latino actor. I'm going to be an actor! . . . *Pa' carajo*
[Damn it].

Urban Latino, No. 22 (1999)

Virgilio Elizondo (San Antonio, Texas)

Priest, scholar, author, professor and television producer, Virgilio Elizondo is the founder and first president of the Mexican American Cultural Center in San Antonio and creator of Nuestra Santa Misa de las Américas, a Mass televised weekly throughout the Spanish-speaking Americas.

From the earliest days of my life, my people introduced me to *Papacito Dios, Jesús, María y los santos* [Daddy God, Jesus, Mary and the saints]. They were very much a part of our immediate and extended family. They were not dogmas to be believed in, but personal friends to visit, converse and even argue with. In our mestizo Christianity—a profound and beautiful blend of Native American religions with Iberian Catholicism—we do not just know about God, but rather we know God personally.

Edward James Olmos, Lea Ibarra and Manuel Monterrey, *Americanos: Latino Life in the United States* (1999)

Jaime Escalante (La Paz, Bolivia, 1930)

After immigration to the United States, Jaime Escalante worked at menial jobs until he earned a degree in mathematics and taught at a high school in the barrio of East Los Angeles. There he inspired hundreds of students to excel. He has won the Presidential Medal for Excellence in Education and the Andrés Bello Prize from the Organization of American States. Escalante's work inspired the film *Stand and Deliver* (1988), starring Edward James Olmos.

[I could] teach rope-climbing to sea lions.

Matt S. Meier, *Notable Latino Americans* (1977)

Martín Espada (Brooklyn, New York, 1957)

Winner of the American Book Award and a nominee for the National Book Critics Circle Award, Martín Espada studied law and later turned to poetry, combining activism and literature.

I'm . . . very aware of a tradition that I come out of, which is the tradition of Latin American poets writing in historical terms.

Christian Science Monitor (March 6, 1991)

I really believe that the best stories come out of history. Either the history of . . . great events, great people, or the history of one's own community, one's own family.

Christian Science Monitor (March 6, 1991)

I am aware of the pitfalls of political poetry . . . but . . . this is not a history that gets told. People are not usually aware that not only blacks but Chicanos were lynched in the American Southwest in appalling numbers, and this was a major way of consolidating power over land. When you talk about how the West was won, you have to talk about that too.

Christian Science Monitor (March 6, 1991)

We are as human beings still capable of being gentle, still capable of kindness, of generosity. Given the cruelty of history, there is virtually no reason in the world any of us should have those qualities. Yet they persist.

Christian Science Monitor (March 6, 1991)

Emilio Estefan Jr. (Unknown place and date of birth)

Leader of the Miami Sound Machine, Emilio Estefan Jr. received six nominations at the first Latin Grammy Awards and was honored as the Latin Academy's Person of the Year (2000). He is also an executive at Sony.

It used to be that people didn't want to hear Latin music or wanted you to change your last name. . . . In order to be successful, you have to be yourself.

New York Times (September 13, 2000)

Gloria Estefan (Havana, Cuba, 1958)

The Cuban-born emigré Gloria Estefan and her Miami Sound Machine, with a blend of salsa, pop and jazz, have sold millions of records to both Hispanics and Anglos. Estefan was probably the first superstar of Latin fusion, or crossover. In 1992 she served as a public delegate for the United States at the United Nations General Assembly.

[When I was a girl] I would lock myself up in my room for hours and just sing. I wouldn't cry—I refused to cry. . . . Music was the only way I had to just let go, so I sang for fun and for . . . catharsis.

Washington Post (July 17, 1988)

We were part of the first wave of Cubans in Miami. When my mother first went to look for an apartment, it was a case of "no children, no pets, no Cubans."

Grace Catalano, *Gloria Estefan* (1991)

Gloria Estefan. Photo by Antoine Verglas. Courtesy of Photofest.

My psychology degree helps me a lot in my career. I constantly auto-
analyze myself.

London Telegraph Magazine (October 22, 1994)

I didn't want to be in the spotlight, didn't desire it. . . . It never crossed
my mind that this is what I'd do the rest of my life. I wanted to be a
psychologist.

Judith Graham (ed.), *Current Biography Yearbook* (1995)

I came from very strong women role models, my mother and my grandmother. . . . She [my mother] always taught you can do anything you
want and . . . never in my house was there any talk of well you are a

woman you can't do this. On the contrary, they were wonderful role models for me in that way.

> Anthony M. DeStefano, *Gloria Estefan: The Pop Superstar from Tragedy to Triumph* (1997)

I am communicating who I am, and who the Hispanics are, and what Latin music means and what we have to offer the world.

> Anthony M. DeStefano, *Gloria Estefan: The Pop Superstar from Tragedy to Triumph* (1997)

If I can take someone's pain away, how can I not help?

> Anthony M. DeStefano, *Gloria Estefan: The Pop Superstar from Tragedy to Triumph* (1997)

We enjoy the ability to choose our future and make it whatever we desire. As Latinos, we can exercise our voting rights to support candidates that care about our concerns. And we *must* get more involved in our government and let our voices be heard.

> *George* (July 1999)

There's no growth without a lot of hard work and a little risk. It's important to me that I continue to grow. There's no point in living life any other way.

> Official Gloria Estefan Web site (August 1999)

Clarissa Pinkola Estés (Indiana, 1943)

Writer and Jungian analyst Clarissa Pinkola Estés was born of Mexican parents but adopted and raised by a Hungarian American family. She has served as executive director of the C. G. Jung Psychoanalytic Institute in Denver, Colorado. Estés is the author of *Women Who Run with the Wolves* (1992).

> People who are twice born as adoptees, especially if they are adopted into another culture, have the special ability to bridge those groups.
>
> *San Francisco Chronicle* (August 2, 1992)

Traditional psychology is often spare or entirely silent about deeper issues important to women; the archetypal, the intuitive, the sexual and cyclical, the ages of women, a woman's way, a woman's knowing, her creative fire.

> *Women Who Run with the Wolves* (1992)

Healthy wolves and healthy women share certain psychic characteristics: keen sensing, playful spirit, and a heightened capacity for devotion. Wolves and women are relational by nature, inquiring, possessed of great endurance and strength. They are deeply intuitive, intensely concerned with their young, their mate, and their pack.

> *Women Who Run with the Wolves* (1992)

Erik Estrada (New York, New York, 1949)

After six years as a star of the television series *CHiPs*, about the California Highway Patrol, Erik Estrada acted in many feature movies. In Mexico he is famous for his roles as a leading man in *telenovelas* (soap operas).

> [When he was starting his career] The music was great, the clothing was wild, the hair was loose and the love was free.
>
> *E!* Web site (2000)

F

Celestino Fernández (Santa Inés, Michoacán, Mexico, 1949)

Vice-president for undergraduate academic affairs at the University of Arizona, Celestino Fernández has published research in many areas of sociology. He also writes poetry and composes *corridos* (Mexican ballads).

Kindergarten in Mexico is almost like second grade here [in the United States]. There was no nonsense, no playtime, you don't take your little mat and have naps or cookies and milk. So that gave me a good start.

Marilyn P. Davis, *Mexican Voices/American Dreams* (1990)

I feel Mexican and I behave American. Inside, my feelings, my values, my attitudes, my beliefs are based in Mexican culture, but my behavior is very American.

Marilyn P. Davis, *Mexican Voices/American Dreams* (1990)

Mexican culture has a certain wisdom I appreciate. My grandfather is *Don* Chema. You can't just call yourself by the title of *Don*. I can't be *Don;* I'm not old enough, I'm not wise enough. Unlike American culture, Mexicans value age. There is respect for someone for simply being older. They don't feel bad if they are ninety, because they are still respected.

Marilyn P. Davis, *Mexican Voices/American Dreams* (1990)

What happens is you become binational and bicultural. You're comfortable in both countries [Mexico and the United States] but never fully integrated in either. You don't want to be, because you know the best world is in the margins, in between, where you can choose and take what is best from each culture.

Marilyn P. Davis, *Mexican Voices/American Dreams* (1990)

Celestino Fernández. Reprinted with permission of Dr. Fernández.

Education opens the door to endless opportunities. I invite you to pass through this door but remember to leave it wide open so that others can follow.

Original quotation for this book (March 2001)

Gigi Fernández (San Juan, Puerto Rico, 1964)

Born Beatriz Fernández and related to the late actor José Ferrer, Gigi Fernández is regarded as one of the greatest doubles players in tennis history. With Mary Joe Fernández (no relation), she won a gold medal at the 1992 Olympics, becoming the first Puerto Rican to accomplish that feat. She repeated with another gold at the 1996 Games. She now works with the Gigi Fernández Charitable Foundation.

[On being the first female professional athlete in Puerto Rico] In a way, it's kind of neat, because it's opening a door for female athletes. . . . Before, it was taboo for a female to make a living out of a sport. Girls are supposed to get married and have kids, so now maybe this opens the door.

Hispanic (July 1988)

My main goal when I retired was to give back.

Then and Now—An Interview with Gigi Fernández Web site (1999)

You have your time, and then you move to make room for the new crop.

Then and Now—An Interview with Gigi Fernández Web site (1999)

You know, I feel very lucky that I don't have to work—financially I saved enough. I was smart enough and had good advisors. Now, I don't have to worry about that, but you still need a reason to wake up in the mornings.

Then and Now—An Interview with Gigi Fernández Web site (1999)

Lisa Fernández (Lakewood, California, 1971)

A four-time NCAA All-America player at UCLA, Lisa Fernández is the most dominant pitcher in woman's softball. She played for the winning American teams in both the 1996 and 2000 Olympic Games. Fernández also plays infield and hits well and has been called the best all-around softball player in the world.

I was lucky not to be raised with the traditional expectations of many Latinas, to become a wife and mother. If it wasn't for the support and sacrifice from my parents . . . I wouldn't be here.

Hispanic (July 31, 1996)

Mary Joe Fernández (Dominican Republic, 1971)

Born María José Fernández, she moved to the United States with her family at the age of six months. Fourteen years later, Mary Joe Fernández was the youngest player ever to win a U.S. Open match. Fernández has won many singles and doubles titles and two Olympic gold medals.

I really love competing and playing in front of a big crowd. Having so many people watching may seem like a lot of pressure, but it helps me play the best I know how. I also enjoy the challenges, mental and physical, of facing an opponent.

All About Mary Joe Fernández Web site (1998)

[On her illnesses and injuries] If it's in the air, I get it.

All About Mary Joe Fernández Web site (1998)

Luis Ferré (Ponce, Puerto Rico, 1904)

Industrialist, politician and philanthropist Luis Ferré held many governmental posts in his native Puerto Rico, including that of governor (1968–72). In 1954 he founded the Luis A. Ferré Foundation, a nonprofit corporation dedicated to artistic, scientific, educational and charitable purposes; it is responsible for the Museo de Arte in Ponce and many other projects. "Don Luis," as he is affectionately known to Puerto Ricans, has received many honorary doctorates and awards.

[His political slogan] *Esto tiene que cambiar* (This must change).

Matt S. Meier, *Notable Latino Americans* (1997)

Rosario Ferré (Ponce, Puerto Rico, 1938)

The most well known Puerto Rican writer of the twentieth century, Rosario Ferré is the author of many novels and collections of short stories. She writes in Spanish and English, sometimes translating her own work. Ferré received the Liberatur Prix at the Frankfurt Book Fair (1992) and was nominated for a National Book Award for her novel *The House on the Lagoon* (1995). She has taught at the University of California at Berkeley, Harvard University, Johns Hopkins University, Rutgers University and the University of Puerto Rico in Río Piedras.

[On translating] It is one of the few instances when one can be dishonest and feel good about it.

Nation (May 5, 1991)

As a Puerto Rican, I'm multilingual, plurilingual, definitely bilingual.

Chicago Tribune (November 1, 1995)

I learned English at seven years of age. . . . English is practical, like binoculars, and precise.

Chicago Tribune (November 1, 1995)

I think writing is a political act. That's enough for me.

Detroit News (October 9, 1996)

We [Puerto Ricans] cannot make up our minds who we are, Hispanics or Americans. We are Hamlets to the nth degree.

Lecture, University of Kentucky (April 2000)

I have compared writing in Spanish to jogging in my Reeboks and writing in English to walking in high heels.

Lecture, University of Kentucky (April 2000)

If I'm writing in English I have to be reading books in English, and if I'm writing in Spanish I have to read books in Spanish.

Lecture, University of Kentucky (April 2000)

America is no longer a melting pot. It's more of a combination plate.
Conversation with the editors (April 2000)

José Ferrer (Santurce, Puerto Rico, 1912–1992)

Known for his resonant voice, bravura and commanding presence on the stage and screen, José Vicente Ferrer de Otero y Cintrón performed leading roles throughout a long career that made him the most famous Hispanic actor of the mid-twentieth century. He won an Oscar for best actor in the film *Cyrano de Bergerac* (1950) and a Gold Medal from the American Academy of Arts and Sciences, and he was inducted into the Theater Hall of Fame.

> [On relationships] At one point or another I think I killed every single person that I loved, and I saw them lying there bleeding before me. . . . I even ran over strangers.
>
> Washington Post (January 27, 1992)

Patrick Flores (Ganado, Texas, 1929)

The son of illiterate sharecroppers, Patrick Flores studied for the priesthood. After serving fourteen years as a parish priest, he was consecrated as auxiliary bishop of San Antonio. Later he became the first Mexican American and the second Latino to be appointed a bishop in the Roman Catholic Church. In 1979 he was named archbishop of San Antonio. Archbishop Flores is famous for his mariachi masses, his Cursillos (short classes) in Spanish and his extensive philanthropic work on behalf of Latinos.

> I think I have a special sensitivity to the poor, not only because I was poor as a child, but because I still am.
>
> Joan Doviak, *Fourteen Beautiful People* (1970)

> I Will Work Not for Myself, but for Others.
>
> Banner displayed at Bishop Flores's consecration (Cinco de mayo, 1972)

> I forgive. In this I have no choice. If I want to be forgiven, I have to forgive.
>
> American Press (July 15, 2000)

Don Francisco (Mario Kreutzberger) (Talca, Chile, 1940)

After hosting the television show *Sábado Gigante* for twenty-four years in Chile, "Don Francisco" decided to expand to thirty other Spanish-speaking countries, including the United States. As an energetic philanthropist through telethon drives, he has helped build six children's

Most Reverend Patrick F. Flores, Archbishop of San Antonio. Reprinted with permission of Archbishop Flores.

hospitals and raised more than $120 million for research. His charitable
work led the United Nations to name him ambassador for UNICEF.

> Latinos will become even more integrated in the coming years. But we'll
> have to work at it. Spanish-language media remind Latinos of what they
> had in their home countries. At the same time, we give them the infor-
> mation they need to be a part of American culture.
>
> *George* (July 1999)

> It was my idea to make the program *(Sábado Gigante)* like soup, to melt
> everything inside. There are interviews, humor, games, singers, every-
> thing—but all in small tablets. People like change. When I started in TV,
> there was no remote control. So the idea was to try and do the remote
> control in people's minds.
>
> *News-Times*, Danbury, Conn., Web site (June 5, 2000)

Carlos Fuentes (Mexico City, Mexico, 1928)

Although he is a member of the Mexican literary elite and could hardly
be called a Chicano, Carlos Fuentes has lived for long periods in the

United States and has often been a spokesperson for our Hispanic minorities.

What the United States does best is to understand itself. What it does worst is understand others.

Time (June 16, 1986)

One wants to tell a story, like Scheherazade [narrator of the *Arabian Nights*], in order not to die. It's one of the oldest urges of mankind. It's a way of stalling death.

Jon Winokur (ed.), *Advice to Writers* (1999)

See them. *Míralos*. They are here. *Están aquí*. They were always here. *Siempre estuvieron aquí*. They arrived before anyone else. *Llegaron antes que nadie. Nadie les pidió pasaportes, visas, tarjetas verdes, señas de identidad.* Nobody asked them for passports, visas, green cards, signs of identity. There were no border guards at [the] Bering Strait when the first men, women, and children crossed over from Asia fifteen to thirty thousand years ago. There were no green cards demanded of the Spanish conquerors, settlers, and missionaries who came into the Southwest and Florida in the sixteenth century. Just as nobody was there to demand entry permits of the Pilgrims who landed on Plymouth Rock in 1620— one hundred years after Cortés discovered California, Ponce de León *la Florida*, and Cabeza de Vaca was shipwrecked on the coast of Texas.

Edward James Olmos, Lea Ibarra and Manuel Monterrey, *Americanos: Latino Life in the United States* (1999)

Recognize yourselves in he or she who are not like you or me.

Edward James Olmos, Lea Ibarra and Manuel Monterrey, *Americanos: Latino Life in the United States* (1999)

How many songs were sung to recall the history of the *mestizo* epic, from Murrieta in California to Pancho Villa in Chihuahua to Martín Fierro in the Pampas, dance bringing together all that makes the body beautiful, rhythmic, delighted to be of the world, in the world, the Indo-Afro-Iberian world where the tango is Andalusian and African, the Mexican *corrido* a descendent of the Castilian *romancero* [ballads], the soulful bolero a child of the Arab love-call, the whole Caribbean carnival of sounds and pleasures derived from all the traditions of the human voice and the human body, its passions, its pains, its longings, its rebellions.

Edward James Olmos, Lea Ibarra and Manuel Monterrey, *Americanos: Latino Life in the United States* (1999)

Daisy Fuentes (Havana, Cuba, 1966)

After living in her native Cuba and in Spain, Daisy Fuentes's family brought her to the United States. She has been an actress, model and television host.

I have a lot of American friends, and for them, it's like, when you turn 18, you're on your own, kid. I think I could be 50 and [my parents] would still be telling me what to do, what to eat and drink your milk.

USA Today (January 13, 1995)

Tina Guerrero Fuentes (San Angelo, Texas, 1949)

Christina Guerrero Fuentes established a reputation as a painter in the 1980s. She is also a teacher and dedicates time to community service. As a tribute to her grandmother, who encouraged her to maintain her Hispanic heritage, she titles her works in Spanish only.

Be true to yourself, first of all. In the long run, you have no one to answer to but you. Do what is artistically important to you.

Artlines (July/August 1987)

G

Andrés Galarraga (Caracas, Venezuela, 1961)

A heavy-hitter in the major leagues, Andrés Galarraga was diagnosed with cancer in his lower back in 1998. After a full year of inactivity and four months of rebuilding in the gym, "The Big Cat" made one of the great recoveries in the history of baseball.

> I wanted to stay alive. I also wanted to be here with my glove and bat. I had to keep myself strong.
>
> *New York Times* (June 28, 2000)

Juan Carlos Galeano (Caqueta, Colombia, 1958)

Poet, scholar and professor Juan Carlos Galeano has taught at Syracuse University and Florida State University. He is the author of several volumes of poetry.

> However you look at it, writing is a recovery. In my case, being an exile, I had to recover my native land. So in my poetry I summoned the place where I was born and the spirits of my people. But recovery is never complete. Although it has the advantage of hindsight, it is always complicated by the present.
>
> Original quotation for this book (June 2001)

> Having children in the United States and Latin America are two different things. In the Hispanic world, the male's participation is small. In the United States, on the other hand, for socioeconomic and cultural reasons, a father has to participate more directly in the care and raising of his children; carrying out tasks that in Latin America, in most cases, are performed by women. This allows a man to share the vital experi-

ence of the early years with his children, which he would otherwise miss.

Original quotation for this book (June 2001)

Rudy Galindo (San Jose, California, 1970)

The first Hispanic to be national men's figure skating champion, Rudy (Valentín Joseph) Galindo overcame a childhood of poverty to become a superb athlete. He turned professional in 1996. In spite of contracting AIDS, he has continued his career in skating.

If you have a dream—if you want something badly enough—and you work hard, it will come true. Look at me; I'm proof.

Matt S. Meier, Notable Latino Americans (1997)

Andy García (Andrés Arturo García-Menéndez) (Havana, Cuba, 1956)

Known for his dark good looks, Andy García is a favorite leading man in Hollywood who has played both heroes and villains. He received an Oscar nomination for best supporting role in *The Godfather Part III* (1990). In addition to being an actor, García is a producer and director.

In the forties and fifties, Havana was the Paris of the Caribbean.

InStyle (January 1999)

I was a banquet waiter at the Beverly Hilton Hotel. You learn a lot when you're in the service industry—the jerks of the world really come to the fore. It's a valuable learning experiences to be in the position where you're of service to someone who sometimes doesn't even know you're there. It's a lesson to learn as a human being—and it's where the root of our problems in society are.

InStyle (January 1999)

I've had my moments of insanity. But there is a certain responsibility to set proper examples for your children, and that influences your choices in every aspect of your life.

InStyle (January 1999)

Cristina García (Havana, Cuba, 1958)

After some ten years as a researcher, reporter and correspondent for the *Boston Globe,* the *Knoxville Journal,* the *New York Times* and *Time* magazine, Cristina García left her career in journalism to write fiction. Her first novel, *Dreaming in Cuban* (1992), was an immediate popular and critical success and was nominated for a National Book Award. García has held a Guggenheim, a Cintas and a Princeton University Hodder Fellowship. She has taught at several universities in California.

> When I was growing up, I was in a virulently anti-Castro home, so Cuba was painted for me as a very monstrous place, an island prison. . . . Writing this helped me to understand my parents and their generation a little better.
>
> *Publishers Weekly* (January 13, 1992)

> There's something in the excavation process that one goes through in creating a book that allowed me to reach areas that I didn't even know existed within myself.
>
> Random House Web site (1997)

> The Cuban aspect of my identity has, to my surprise, become my wellspring. It is now an indelible, strong and very visceral part of my identity.
>
> Random House Web site (1997)

> You need to carve out, and protect, uninterrupted time for yourself on a daily basis. Getting in the habit of taking time seriously is important because the time is the ultimate factory for these novels.
>
> Random House Web site (1997)

> You have to be comfortable with solitude because novel writing is not a collaborative process. Party animals need not apply.
>
> Random House Web site (1997)

> [On her former husband, whom she considers to be her best friend] Once in a while we talk about "what might have been," but the truth is that, as husband and wife, we probably would have killed each other. What we have now is the perfect relationship—it has everything and nothing to do with the rest of my life. When I look into the distant future, I see us rolling into the sunset together. In our wheelchairs.
>
> *O* (Oprah magazine) (November 2000)

Eric García (Unknown place and date of birth)

Raised in Florida, Eric García studied at Cornell University and the University of Southern California. While working as a screenwriter, he wrote his first novel, *Anonymous Rex: A Detective Story* (2000). This book stood the mystery genre on its ear by creating a private eye who is a velociraptor disguised as a human. García is working on a movie deal and a prequel to the novel. Its sequel is *Casual Rex* (2001).

> I got the idea [for a dinosaur-detective] while watching a documentary (about dinosaurs) on television. . . . I'm trying to entertain as many people as possible.
>
> *Lexington Herald-Leader* (January 2, 2000)

The dinosaurs didn't die out. They just went into hiding. That's the genesis of *Anonymous Rex*.

Anonymous Rex Web site (January 2000)

Every single one [noir movie] is a morality tale, filled with bright, bold characters and dialogue so snappy it'll bite your ear off.

Anonymous Rex Web site (January 2000)

I tend to devour authors, in the sense that once I read one book which I enjoy, I go through their catalogs with a fervor bordering on obsession.

Anonymous Rex Web site (January 2000)

[Advice for young writers] There is this, and only this: Blank screen, one chair, your butt. Do with it what you will.

Anonymous Rex Web site (January 2000)

Write when you feel it. Write when your fingers don't move fast enough to get the words in your head onto the paper. And if you want, write when you don't feel it, as well.

Anonymous Rex Web site (January 2000)

Guy García (Los Angeles, California, 1955)

Journalist and novelist Guy García studied at the University of California, Berkeley, and at Columbia. He has published in *Elle*, *Rolling Stone*, *Time* and other magazines. García is author of the novel *Skin Deep* (1988).

Celebrities are instant icons.

Time (June 29, 1987)

Jerry García (San Francisco, California, 1942–1995)

From 1966 until his death, singer, guitarist and composer Jerry (Jerome John) García performed with his famous Grateful Dead, one of the most successful touring bands of all time.

To the kids today, The Grateful Dead represents America, . . . being able to go out and have an adventure.

Washington Post (August 10, 1995)

Sergio García (Castellón, Spain, 1980)

Known as "*El Niño*" and "the next Tiger Woods," golfer Sergio García started playing at three, won a club championship at twelve, made the first cut in a European P.G.A. event at fourteen and won his first professional tournament at seventeen, while still an amateur. In 1999 he won the Irish Open.

I probably hit it [the golf ball] so far because of the way I swing. When I was young, I was so short that I had to swing very fast. Like Indiana Jones snapping a bullwhip.

USA Today (July 16, 1998)

I always think under par. You have to believe in yourself.

USA Today (July 16, 1998)

I have given a lot of things up, but when you want to do something with your life, that is always the way.

Golf World (April 2, 1999)

I just want to be recognized as Sergio García, not the European Tiger Woods.

Golf Plus Web site (May 20, 1999)

Magic shots. . . . It's something you can't teach. These shots are something that's inside you and you have to see them in your imagination.

Sports Illustrated (September 27, 1999)

[When asked if he was frightened by competing with the world's greatest golfers] No, I'm not.

New Yorker (October 18 & 25, 1999)

Nomar Garciaparra (Whittier, California, 1973)

Half Mexican and half Egyptian, Nomar Garciaparra was both American League Rookie of the Year and Most Valuable Player in 1997. He led the American League in batting in 1999.

I enjoy the game every day, and that's all that is important to me. I take it for all it's worth. At the same time, I understand it could all be gone tomorrow.

Current Biography (June 2000)

You have to go out there and work hard and contribute day in and day out to try and win.

Current Biography (June 2000)

Dagoberto Gilb (Los Angeles, California, 1950)

Although he had earned B.A. and M.A. degrees from the University of California, Santa Barbara, Dagoberto Gilb worked as a journeyman carpenter for years before breaking into the literary world with *The Magic of Blood* (1994). This collection of short stories was a finalist for the PEN/Faulkner Award and won first prizes from both the Hemingway Foundation and the Texas Institute of Letters. Gilb has won a creative writing fellowship from the National Endowment for the Arts.

Write from the gut and soul. Spill it. Write from *las alturas* [the heights] and from *hoyos* [the depths] (avoid cheap, italicized, affected use of Spanish words). Don't offer excuses, explanations, apologies, *apologias* (the Latin).

anq (American Notes & Queries) (Spring 1997)

Try to please God or the Virgin and not others (well, Others). But privately. As in silent prayer.

anq (American Notes & Queries) (Spring 1997)

You will quit your day job; if you're a writer, you'll be fired soon enough anyway.

anq (American Notes & Queries) (Spring 1997)

If you want to be The Leader of the People, if you want to be a Saint, if you want to be The Guru, please don't pretend to be first of all a writer. Unless you're dead.

anq (American Notes & Queries) (Spring 1997)

Don't write for public acclaim. Unless you need the money. Be honest that is all. Good luck, by the way.

anq (American Notes & Queries) (Spring 1997)

Arlene F. Gillespie (San Juan, Puerto Rico, 1936)

Born to a Hispanic father and a British mother, Arlene Fullana Gillespie is an economist, public servant and activist. She has served as executive director of the Office of Latino Affairs in Washington, D.C., and has worked with the National Puerto Rican Coalition.

I felt some kind of claustrophobia living in Puerto Rico. I loved the island, but I considered that it was too small for me. I longed to spread my wings in a larger territory, that of the mainland United States. Sometimes I felt nostalgia, but I knew I was capable of doing more.

Diane Telgen and Jim Kamp (eds.), *Notable Hispanic American Women* (1993)

Roberto Goizueta (Havana, Cuba, 1931–1999)

After studying chemical engineering at Yale University, Roberto Goizueta began working at the Coca-Coca Company, eventually rising to chief executive officer and chairman of the board. He was known internationally for his humanitarianism, especially in his role as founder of the Points of Light Initiative Foundation. He received many awards, including the Ellis Island Medal of Honor and held honorary doctorates at several universities.

Roberto Goizueta. Courtesy of Mrs. Roberto Goizueta and The Goizueta Foundation.

One's personal commitments are much more important than the truth or falsehood of one's position.

Mark Pendergrast, *For God, Country, and Coca Cola* (2000)

It is a good sign that human beings almost always act in their own interest.

Mark Pendergrast, *For God, Country, and Coca Cola* (2000)

Lefty Gómez (Vernon Louis) (Rodeo, California, 1909)

The famous pitcher for the New York Yankees from 1930 to 1942, Lefty Gómez pitched in five World Series with a perfect 6–0 record. Also known as "Goofy" and "The Gay Castillion," he was elected to the Baseball Hall of Fame in 1972.

If you don't throw it, they can't hit it. [Known as "Gómez's Law"]

Lawrence J. Peter, *Peter's Quotations: Ideas for Our Time* (1977)

Guillermo Gómez-Peña (Mexico City, Mexico, 1955)

Chicano writer and performing artist Guillermo Gómez-Peña is the author of *Warrior for Gringostroika* (1993), which contains the artistic manifesto "The Border Is," quoted here. His *The New World Border* (1996) won the

American Book Award. Gómez-Peña has won a MacArthur Foundation grant.

> Border culture means boycott, complot [= plot], ilegalidad, clandestinidad, contrabando, transgresión, desobediencia binacional [binational disobedience]. . . . But it also means transcultural friendship and collaboration among races, sexes, and generations. But it also means to practice creative appropriation, expropriation, and subversion of dominant cultural forms. But it also means a multiplicity of voices away from the center, different geo-cultural relations among more culturally akin regions. . . . But it also means *regresar* [to go back], *volver y partir:* to return and depart once again. . . . But it also means a new terminology for new hybrid identities and métiers constantly metamorphosizing. . . . But it also means to look at the past and the future at the same time.
>
> *Warrior for Gringostroika* (1993)

> The insidious colonial tendencies we have internalized—and that express themselves in sadistic competition for money and attention, political cannibalism, and moral distrust—must be overcome. We must realize that we are not each other's enemies and that the true enemy is currently enjoying our divisiveness.
>
> *Warrior for Gringostroika* (1993)

Mary Gonzales (Unknown place and date of birth)

Mary Gonzales is cofounder and associate director of a neighborhood organization in Chicago.

> Think about the guy who works in a factory. He's on the assembly line. He's nobody. He doesn't do the kind of work that's ever gonna get him recognition. Take that same person and he's a key leader in the parish or in a union. Suddenly that same man, who from Monday to Friday stands on the assembly line at General Motors and is a nobody, is somebody over here. People look to him. He makes a difference and he knows it. He counts.
>
> Studs Terkel, *The Great Divide* (1988)

Pancho (Richard) Gonzales (Los Angeles, California, 1928–1995)

The son of immigrants from Mexico, Pancho Gonzales was a self-taught tennis player. He was singles champion at Forest Hills in 1948 and the top singles player in professional tennis from 1954 through 1962. Gonzales coached the U.S. Davis Cup team in 1968 and is a member of the Tennis Hall of Fame.

> [I will play] as long as I can walk on a court.
>
> Joan Doviak, *Fourteen Beautiful People* (1970)

Rebecca Gonzales (Laredo, Texas, 1946)

The daughter of migrant field workers, poet Rebecca Gonzales grew up in Texas and other states. She has worked as a high school English teacher and a journalist.

I remember asking my father when I was small what he was going to give me for my birthday. He said, *"¿Qué quieres que te dé, hija, más que mi corazón?"* [What more can I give you, daughter, than my heart?]. After that, I remember asking just to hear the same answer.

> Wolfgang Binder (ed.), *Partial Autobiographies: Interviews with Twenty Chicano Poets* (1985)

Rodolfo Corky Gonzáles (Denver, Colorado, 1928)

The widely known author of the epic poem *I Am Joaquín* (1967), Corky Gonzáles has also been a prizefighter, activist, politician and community organizer. He was once a leading spokesman for a movement in favor of a national Chicano homeland called Aztlán.

There are no revolutions without poets.

> Introduction, *I Am Joaquín* (1972)

I'd rather be out in the front line of the revolution than hiding in a closet.

> John C. Hammerback, Richard J. Jensen and José Ángel Gutiérrez, *A War of Words: Chicano Protest in the 1960s and 1970s* (1985)

Every spring and summer as a boy, I worked in the fields. Every fall and winter I lived in the city slums.

> John C. Hammerback, Richard J. Jensen and José Ángel Gutiérrez, *A War of Words: Chicano Protest in the 1960s and 1970s* (1985)

I became a fighter [boxer] because it was the fastest way to get out of the slaughterhouse. So I thought.

> John C. Hammerback, Richard J. Jensen and José Ángel Gutiérrez, *A War of Words: Chicano Protest in the 1960s and 1970s* (1985)

Aztlán may be a myth or it may be a real place, but it always stands for the idea of a homeland, of freedom from that which we are not, of reclaiming what we are.

> John C. Hammerback, Richard J. Jensen and José Ángel Gutiérrez, *A War of Words: Chicano Protest in the 1960s and 1970s* (1985)

Chicano history predates Plymouth Rock and Jamestown. . . . When we start relating to what we are and where we come from we will start becoming proud of ourselves.

> John C. Hammerback, Richard J. Jensen and José Ángel Gutiérrez, *A War of Words: Chicano Protest in the 1960s and 1970s* (1985)

Corky Gonzáles (taken at the time of the "courthouse raid" incident in Tierra Amarilla, New Mexico, 1967). Courtesy of the Center for Southwest Research, General Library, University of New Mexico.

Sylvia Alicia Gonzales (Arizona, 1943)

Educator, activist and author Sylvia Alicia Gonzales has served as executive director of the National Association of Bilingual Education and has worked for both the Mexican American Women's National Association and the National Women's Political Caucus.

> As a minority in this country, caught between two worlds of language, culture, and history, it was important to have a voice. My own predicament inspired me to seek, understand, interpret the broader experience of humankind in order to find my place in the world. I grew to love people, cultures, differences, in a way that I had not been loved or accepted.
>
> *Contemporary Authors* (1979)

I traveled to Latin America seeking my roots, Europe in search of my universality, and the barrios of the United States to share with my people.

Contemporary Authors (1979)

If we aspire to leadership, then let it be the leadership of cooperation and group consciousness to change our destinies.

Nuestro (August/September 1981)

Henry B. González (San Antonio, Texas, 1916)

A longtime Democratic representative from Texas, Henry B. González had a unique reputation for honesty and independence. He chaired many important committees in Congress, including banking, finance and urban affairs. In addition to being the first Mexican American congressman from his home state, the beloved and feared "Henry B." was also the first Mexican American in more than a century to be elected to the Texas Senate. González contributed to the San Antonio *Express-News* and *La Prensa* (in Spanish).

This is my land. I'm part of it. Why should I be an alien? I was born here.

Joan Doviak, *Fourteen Beautiful People* (1970)

Well, what's the difference? Mexican, Negro, what have you? The assault on the inward dignity of man, which our society protects, has been made. . . . For whom does the bell toll? You, the white man, think it tolls for the Negro. I say, the bell tolls for you. It's ringing for us all.

John C. Hammerback, Richard J. Jensen and José Ángel Gutiérrez, *A War of Words: Chicano Protest in the 1960s and 1970s* (1985)

I walked through the mud of San Antonio politics, I walked through the mud of state politics in Austin. And for thirty years, I've walked through the mud in Washington, D.C., and I still haven't gotten the tips of my shoes dirty.

Current Biography Yearbook (1993)

Jackie Guerra (San Diego, California, 1967)

The daughter of immigrants from Mexico, comedienne Jackie Guerra grew up in Los Angeles. After studying at Yale University and the University of California, San Diego, she worked as a union organizer, then started her career as a comedienne. With the situation comedy *First Time Out*, Guerra became the first Latina to star in her own prime-time series. She has also appeared in films.

Avoid excessive housework.

Tampa Tribune (June 1, 1996)

Dan Guerrero (Tucson, Arizona, 1940)

A leading figure in the booming field of Hispanic television in the United States, Dan Guerrero has worked for both of the major Spanish-language networks, Univisión and Telemundo, as well as ABC. He has been twice honored by the Imagen Foundation for bringing positive views of Latino culture to the screen. Guerrero remains active in the Hispanic community, producing fundraisers for the Bilingual Foundation of the Arts, the United Farm Workers Union and Latino students. He is son of the great musician Lalo Guerrero.

As a television producer, I'm constantly amazed at how uninformed the industry is about the U.S. Latino. We are a richly diverse people, but to

Dan Guerrero. Courtesy of Mr. Guerrero.

Hollywood, there is seemingly no difference between an Argentine, a Mexican or a Puerto Rican. That's why you'll still see Mexican sarape curtains hanging in the home of a Brazilian character on a TV sitcom. But, at the same time, Hollywood has figured out the differences in the Asian community and is sensitive not to confuse the Korean, Japanese or Chinese cultures with one another. What does that say?

Original quotation for this book (September 2001)

Lalo Guerrero (Tucson, Arizona, 1916)

Known as the "father of Chicano music," Eduardo "Lalo" Guerrero has enjoyed a career spanning four decades. He is the composer of more than 200 songs. Guerrero was the first Chicano honored at the White House with a National Medal for the Arts and has been declared a "national folk treasure" by the Smithsonian Institution.

Funny things happen when you try.

The Lalo Story Web site (2001)

Lalo Guerrero. Courtesy of Mr. Guerrero.

Anything is possible in this country.

The Lalo Story Web site (2001)

When I first met him [labor activist César Chávez], in Delano, I was on the road with my band. . . . César would come [to the clubs] with his friends, looking for girls. He'd say "Lalo, they're gonna be picking onions over in Sacramento Valley" or "Lalo, they're gonna be picking strawberries in Bakersfield," and the pickers were mostly Chicanos, so he'd tip me to where they'd be, we'd go there to play, and sure enough, there would be a lot of people to see us.

National Endowment for the Arts Art Forms Web site (2001)

I love to be around musicians, around music. I don't tell myself, "Keep active" or anything, I just love what I'm doing, and lately I've been getting recognition, which feels very good. I wouldn't try to stop something that feels so good.

National Endowment for the Arts Art Forms Web site (2001)

Luis Guzmán (Puerto Rico)

Luis Guzmán is an actor who has performed in many American movies.

I certainly want to keep working my craft, working my art, because I love what I do. But, to me, the most important thing is being a good father and friend to my children. Hopefully, I'm setting an example to other Latino men as a father and as an actor. I can step into the world of being an artist and I can step out of that world and be Papi. I love that.

Latina (December 1999)

When I do movies, I don't want you to like me. I either want you to love me or hate me. Liking me is not enough, you know. Because when you really hate someone in a role you remember that. You love someone in a role, you remember that.

Latina (December 1999)

Sandra Guzmán (Puerto Rico)

After living in the fishing village of Las Cucharas, Puerto Rico, Sandra Guzmán's family moved to New Jersey, where she graduated from Rutgers University. She worked as a journalist for *El Diario/La Prensa* and later as a producer for Telemundo, for whom she won an Emmy Award. Guzmán then became editor of *Latina* magazine.

Imagine, a so-called nutritious program that tells me I can't eat *arroz con pollo* [chicken and rice Caribbean style] or *pasteles* [meat pies]. As far as I'm concerned, that's anti-Latino, and I won't go for it. *Nuestra comida* [our cooking] is chock-full of nutrition, so what are those "experts" talking about, anyway?

Latina (April 1998)

H

Christy Haubegger (Houston, Texas, 1968)

Founder, president and publisher of *Latina* magazine, Christy Haubegger grew up as the adopted daughter of Anglo parents who gave her Spanish lessons from an early age and instilled in her a strong sense of her Hispanic heritage.

> [When she was a teenager] You never saw anyone with brown eyes in *Seventeen* magazine.
>
> *Texas Monthly* (September 1997)

> This quiet *revolución* can be traced back to the bloodless coup of 1992, when salsa outsold ketchup for the first time. Having toppled the leadership in the condiment category, we set our sights even higher.
>
> *Newsweek* (July 12, 1999)

> The Latinization of this country will pay off. . . . I, for one, look forward to the pivotal moment in our history when all American men finally know how to dance. Latin music will no longer be found in record stores under FOREIGN and romance will bloom again. Our children will ask us what it was like to dance without a partner.
>
> *Newsweek* (July 12, 1999)

Salma Hayek (Coatzacoalcos, Mexico, 1968)

Before coming to Hollywood, Salma Hayek acted in several plays, soap operas and films in Mexico. Her movie credits include *Mi Vida Loca* (1994), *Desperado* (1995), *Wild Wild West* (1999) and *Frida* (2002).

> I aim for a lifetime of movies.
>
> *Interview* (February 1997)

When I got to Hollywood, being Mexican was considered so uncool.
. . . If I have my way, that's going to change.

Time (April 14, 1997)

I'm pretty much an abstract figure that people can project their fantasies
on; it's pretty much what we all are, otherwise we wouldn't be stars,
and people wouldn't be interested.

Elle (April 2000)

I'm well aware most of the audience prefers me a certain way, at least
when I'm out in public. What way? Dressed as a nun, of course. Okay,
maybe not.

Elle (April 2000)

When I first came to Hollywood, one of the stereotypes I encountered
. . . was that Latinas were tacky and had no sense of style. That wasn't
my reality, it's not what I knew, so I made it a task for myself to change
that.

Elle (April 2000)

Rita Hayworth (Brooklyn, New York, 1918–1987)

Born Margarita Carmen Cansino into a family of Spanish-Irish-English
ancestry, Rita Hayworth became Hollywood's "sex goddess" of the 1930s
and 1940s. Her tempestuous life included marriages to actor-director Orson Welles, millionaire Aly Khan and singer Dick Haymes.

I like having my picture taken and being a glamorous person. Sometimes when I find myself getting impatient, I just remember the times I
cried my eyes out because nobody wanted to take my picture.

New York Times (May 16, 1987)

[On Orson Welles] I'm tired of being a 25-percent wife.

Time (May 25, 1987)

[On Orson Welles] I just can't take his genius anymore.

Diane Telgen and Jim Kamp (eds.), *Notable Hispanic American Women* (1993)

Ester Hernández (San Joaquin Valley, California, 1944)

Using murals, pastels and printmaking, artist Ester Hernández is an activist in the Chicano art movement. She has exhibited her work throughout the United States and in Latin America, Africa and Europe.

My background has taught me that we Chicanos must continually strive
for beauty and spirituality. This beauty—found in both nature and the
arts—is the seed that uplifts our spirit and nourishes our souls.

Joseph M. Palmisano (ed.), *Notable Hispanic American Women*, Book II (1998)

Orlando "El Duque" Hernández (Villa Clara, Cuba, 1965)

A pitcher for the Cuban national baseball team, Orlando Hernández was banned from the sport by the Cuban government when his half brother Liván Hernández defected to the United States. In 1997 "El Duque" escaped the island on a small sailboat and became a star pitcher for the New York Yankees.

> [On his escape from Cuba and success in major league baseball] I hope [Fidel Castro] watches me and is pulling the hair out of his beard.
>
> *Sports Illustrated* (August 17, 1998)

> You pitch until you die. When you cannot pitch with your arm, you go with your heart.
>
> *Sports Illustrated* (August 17, 1998)

> [On his childhood in Cuba] I was a very happy person because my family worked very hard. . . . I didn't have the best material things in the world, but in my heart my life was the best in the world.
>
> *Cigar Aficionado* (April 1999)

> I started playing at about seven years old. I would not cry for food when I was young, but I did cry for baseball.
>
> *Cigar Aficionado* (April 1999)

Orlando "El Duque" Hernández. Courtesy of the National Baseball Hall of Fame Library, Cooperstown, N.Y.

[As a child] I slept with my bat and ball and glove.

Cigar Aficionado (April 1999)

[On his escape from Cuba] This was the work of God, because on top of everything the water was very calm and the winds were in our favor. So I expected the good Lord's hand was there. We were all thinking about what we had left behind, our families, and about everything that awaits you on the frontier.

Cigar Aficionado (April 1999)

I've been enjoying democracy and freedom. Here no one can tell me what to say. It has changed my life already.

Current Biography (April 2000)

Since [I was] a young boy, I've always dreamed about the New York Yankees.

Current Biography (April 2000)

Hope. . . . That's what I have for breakfast every morning.

Lexington Herald-Leader (May 20, 2001)

Inside every Cuban there's a ballplayer waiting to get out.

Steve Fainaru and Ray Sánchez, *The Duke of Havana* (2001)

I had one pair of pants that I called "the Weeklies." . . . Why did I call them "the Weeklies"? Because I wore the same pants every day. I had another pair of pants that I called "the Big Saturdays." I wore them every Saturday to go to a party.

Steve Fainaru and Ray Sánchez, *The Duke of Havana* (2001)

I know the prettiest word in the world is *money*. But I believe that words like *loyalty* and *patriotism* are very beautiful as well.

Steve Fainaru and Ray Sánchez, *The Duke of Havana* (2001)

I had a job to do, not only for me but for my family, my friends, for all Latinos and all Cubans.

Steve Fainaru and Ray Sánchez, *The Duke of Havana* (2001)

¡Todo bien! ["Everything's okay!" Hernández's signature greeting and farewell].

Inés Hernández-Ávila (Galveston, Texas, 1947)

Inés Hernández-Ávila is a writer and activist. Her work reflects her dual heritage as a Chicana and a Nez Percé.

To be revolutionary is to be original, to know where we came from, to validate what is ours and help it to flourish, the best of what is ours, of our beginnings, our principles, and to leave behind what no longer serves us.

Mary Biggs, *Women's Words: The Columbia Book of Quotations by Women* (1996)

Carolina Herrera (Caracas, Venezuela, 1939)

María Carolina Josefina Pacanins y Nino is a socialite-turned-designer. She began her professional career under her married name of Carolina Herrera. She won the 1987 MODA Award for top Hispanic designer.

[I] changed from being a mother with nothing to do but arrange flowers and parties to being a professional who works twelve hours a day at the office.

Newsweek (June 30, 1986)

I didn't dream about being a designer, but I always loved clothes. I grew up with three sisters who also loved clothes, and my grandmother was a great beauty.

New York Times (January 4, 1994)

I don't do grunge. I don't do see-through. I think women should look elegant.

New York Times (January 4, 1994)

I have time for everything, even time to be alone.

New York Times (January 4, 1994)

To survive in this business, you have to believe in something, stay with it, and be secure about it. If you want to shock the public, you are out of control and about to become a fashion victim.

Judith Graham (ed.), *Current Biography Yearbook* (1996)

I think it's important to be always very soigné, well groomed, at your best. And why not? That's why we are women.

Judith Graham (ed.), *Current Biography Yearbook* (1996)

Juan Felipe Herrera (Fowler, California, 1948)

The son of migrant workers, Juan Felipe Herrera is a Chicano poet. He belonged to the *indigenista* group and has been a teacher.

We may be contained, our condition may be very difficult, but we will cut through the wire, we will eventually emerge, and grow, and disperse our own sense of being, our own perfume.

Wolfang Binder (ed.), *Partial Autobiographies: Interviews with Twenty Chicano Poets* (1985)

Paloma Herrera (Buenos Aires, Argentina, 1975)

A dancer from the age of seven, Paloma Herrera studied in her native Argentina and at the School of American Ballet in the United States. She is principal dancer for the American Ballet Theatre in New York City.

> You know, other little girls at seven or eight don't really know what they want. But I knew right away. From the first day I knew I wanted to be a dancer and there was no way I was going to change my mind.
>
> *Current Biography* (April 2000)

> My life is on the stage.
>
> *Current Biography* (April 2000)

> I love to make art on the stage, not just technique. That's what I always work for—to make something good happen onstage.
>
> *Current Biography* (April 2000)

> I'm full of projects and I'm always willing to try something new. I don't plan my life, but I feel I have always done what I love.
>
> *Current Biography* (April 2000)

María Hinojosa (Mexico City, Mexico, 1961)

Journalist, correspondent, producer and researcher María Hinojosa worked for CNN and National Public Radio before being named the host of *Latino USA*, a radio journal of news and culture. She was the first Hispanic to host a live televison show in prime time. In 1995 *Hispanic Business* magazine named Hinojosa one of the 100 most influential Latinos. In 1999 she won the Rubén Salazar Award from the National Council of La Raza.

> Growing up as a Mexican immigrant in Chicago, I always had the experience of being the "other." I was the other among my mostly white friends in the states but I was also the other when I would go back to Mexico and my younger cousins would tease me about being an "americana."
>
> *Current Biography* (February 2001)

> Feeling as an outsider helped me identify with others who might be seen in the same way. Feeling that my "voice" was never really important, I saw myself in others who were voiceless as well. In my work as a journalist and as an outsider I hope to give that voice back to the voiceless. All of society's voices and perspectives are legitimate and important. We might not like what we hear but we have a responsibility to listen.
>
> *Current Biography* (February 2001)

Tish Hinojosa (1955)

The youngest of thirteen children born to immigrant parents, Tish Hinojosa went on to become a singer and songwriter who combines country-western, folk and *conjunto* (group) sounds. She has worked on behalf of the National Association for Bilingual Education as well as the National Latino Children's Agenda.

> [On her first guitar] It was just the $20 guitar you get down [in Mexico] at the *mercado* [market]. But I was really, really proud, and I still have that guitar.
>
> *Dallas Morning News* (May 29, 1994)

> So many of the singer-songwriters just don't fit into niches in Nashville or in pop music anymore. I guess I'm one of those. But I feel like I'm in good company, because I like a lot of people that are in the same crack that I'm in.
>
> *Los Angeles Times* (November 26, 1992)

Rolando Hinojosa-Smith (Mercedes, Texas, 1929)

Son of a Mexican American father and an Anglo mother, novelist Rolando Hinojosa-Smith has a remarkable command of both English and Spanish, writing equally well in both languages. He has won several awards, including the Premio Casa de las Américas for his *Klail City: A Novel* (1976), the most prestigious literary prize in Latin America. Hinojosa-Smith's work is better known in Latin America and Europe than in his own country. He has taught and served as a dean at Texas A & M and the University of Texas. Under the pseudonym P. Galindo, he wrote the *Devil's Dictionary* (1973) and *The Mexican American Devil's Dictionary* (1976).

> AIR. One of the four natural elements; the other three being space, freedom, and friendship. For many Chicanos, air is the first meal of the day.
>
> *Devil's Dictionary, El Grito* (Spring 1973)

> AMERICAN DREAM, THE. A myth. Also, an all-white professional basketball team.
>
> *Devil's Dictionary, El Grito* (Spring 1973)

> BARBECUE. A religious gathering wherein Chicanos are invited to participate . . . [in election years]. The barbecue meat is cooked by hot air.
>
> *Devil's Dictionary, El Grito* (Spring 1973)

> BRIBERY. Interchangeable with "apple pie" and "mother."
>
> *Devil's Dictionary, El Grito* (Spring 1973)

Rolando Hinojosa-Smith. Courtesy of the Office of Public Affairs, University of Texas.

CROPS. Sustenance for the many picked by the few who are paid little by the big, who are even fewer.

Devil's Dictionary, El Grito (Spring 1973)

G.O.B. Initials designating a Good Old Boy. (Sometimes confused with S.O.B.) Most Good Old Boys played high school football, married the cheerleaders, joined the Jaycees and are now forty pounds overweight.

Devil's Dictionary, El Grito (Spring 1973)

HONESTY. A nonmarketable item.

The Mexican American Devil's Dictionary, Revista Chicano-Riqueña (Fall 1976)

MEXICAN AMERICAN. Chicano, Hispano, Latino, Mexican, Latinoamericano, Boy, Legless war vet, Spanish-surnamed, Spanish American,

Spanish-speaking American. People who refuse to go back to where they came from, namely, Texas, New Mexico, Arizona, Colorado, California, etc.

Devil's Dictionary, El Grito (Spring 1973)

SHOCK, CULTURE. The startling realization that Chicanos possess sensitivity, and intelligence.

Devil's Dictionary, El Grito (Spring 1973)

TEXAS. A place where Mexicans should be seen and not heard. . . . The complete story of Texas and its achievements has been compiled by J. Frank Dobie, John Wayne, and Cantinflas.

Devil's Dictionary, El Grito (Spring 1973)

XENOPHOBIA. An illness which disappears with the appearance of profit.

The Mexican American Devil's Dictionary, Revista Chicano-Riqueña (Fall 1976)

Home to Texas, our Texas
That slice of hell, heaven,
Purgatory and land of our Fathers.

Rolando Hinojosa-Smith, *Korean Love Songs* (1980)

[In the Rio Grande Valley] There are no legendary heroes here: these people go to the bathroom, sneeze, wipe their noses, raise their families, know how to die without a cent, to give in a little with difficulty and (like green wood) to resist giving up.

Klail City: A Novel (1987)

I come from a family of readers; my parents, when not engaged in reading individually, took turns reading to each other. And, you could always find my brothers and sisters with their noses in some book or other.

anq (American Notes & Queries) (Spring 1997)

Languages and the putting together of words fascinated me then, and the fascination continues, whether the words are put together by other writers or by what I have come up with, from time to time.

anq (American Notes & Queries) (Spring 1997)

Readers often ask which language I prefer [Spanish or English]; the answer is always the same: "My worry is not which language I prefer to use, my worry is if I have anything to write about or not."

anq (American Notes & Queries) (Spring 1997)

An education, for those without land or property, is not only important, it is essential. Too, an education presents the opportunity to know not only yourself, but also to know where you come from, and, best of all, to lead those who are beginning their education.

Original quotation for this book (January 2000)

Dolores Huerta (Dawson, New Mexico, 1930)

A folk hero in the Mexican American community who is portrayed on murals and sung in *corridos* (ballads), Dolores Huerta cofounded with labor activist César Chávez the organization that would become the United Farm Workers of America. She is the mother of eleven children and has been a strike organizer, boycott and contract negotiator, lobbyist and official of the UFWA.

I realized one day that as a teacher I couldn't do anything for the kids who came to school barefoot and hungry.

Regeneración, Vol. 1, No. 11 (1971)

My grandfather used to call me seven tongues . . . because I always talked so much.

Diane Telgen and Jim Kamp (eds.), *Notable Hispanic Women* (1993)

I think we [United Farm Workers of America] brought to the world, the United States anyway, the whole idea of boycotting as a nonviolent tactic. I think we showed the world that nonviolence can work to make social change.

Diane Telgen and Jim Kamp (eds.), *Notable Hispanic Women* (1993)

People thought we were crazy. They asked, "How are you going to organize farm workers? They are poor, powerless immigrants. They don't have any money and they can't vote."

Salt Lake City Tribune (October 15, 1996)

My mother was a strong woman and she didn't favor my brothers. There was no idea that men were superior. At home we all shared in the household tasks. I never had to cook for my brothers or do their clothes like in many traditional Mexican families.

Susan Ferris and Richard Sandoval, *The Fight in the Fields* (1997)

I knew what it was like to send kids to school with shoes that had holes.

Susan Ferris and Richard Sandoval, *The Fight in the Fields* (1997)

I

Abdón Ibarra (Laredo, Texas, 1946)

The son of illegal immigrants from Mexico, Abdón Ibarra has worked with migrant farm workers and immigrants for more than thirty years.

> U.S. immigration policy does not take into account the economic contributions of these hard-working and resourceful people [immigrants from Mexico]. It harms not only the so-called illegals but also the society that benefits so much from their labor.
>
> *Lexington Herald-Leader* (April 9, 2000)

> So many parts of these workers' lives are controlled by their immigration status that they live in the shadows of the night. They shop in the evenings under the protective mantel of the dark. They socialize in crowded apartments so as to not inconvenience anyone. They listen to their music in seclusion, almost apologetically.
>
> *Lexington Herald-Leader* (April 9, 2000)

> Open the doors to your churches so that immigrants, too, can worship. Offer a helping hand when you see them in need, brighten their day with a cordial smile. But most of all, honor the differences and recognize the similarities in work ethic, family values and the aspirations for a better life and the blessings of freedom.
>
> *Lexington Herald-Leader* (April 9, 2000)

Enrique Iglesias (Madrid, Spain, 1975)

Raised in Spain and the United States, Enrique Iglesias recorded his first album without his famous father Julio's knowledge and soon became a leading singer in his own right. A composer as well as a performer, he travels the world giving concerts with his entourage of sixty-five people.

My dream is for my music to be heard in every corner of the world. I'd like to be in an elevator in Hong Kong and hear my songs.

New York Times Magazine (January 21, 1996)

Please do not introduce me as the son of Julio Iglesias. I'm very proud of my father, but when you read *Billboard* now, you see *Enrique Iglesias*.

People (April 22, 1996)

The day nothing happens to me, that I'm not approached at a restaurant for an autograph or woken up at 4 A.M. to have my picture taken, is the day that I'm finished.

El Paso Herald-Post (April 3, 1997)

When I was seven, I'd kneel in bed and pray I'd be a singer.

Billboard (July 19, 1997)

[On his Hispanic background] I gotta remember something—what got me here was Spanish.

Clifford Thompson (ed.), *Current Biography Yearbook* (1999)

I write late at night. . . . I probably write until seven in the morning, and then I wake up around twelve o'clock and . . . if I read it and it doesn't accomplish what I want, if it doesn't express what I want to say, then I just throw it away.

Urban Latino, No. 22 (1999)

If you talk about Marc Anthony or Ricky Martin [other Hispanic singers], they're great. I'm a big fan of them, but they're Tropical. I'm from Spain. I'm much more Mediterranean. There's much more guitar in my music. There's a difference between Salsa and Flamenco.

Urban Latino, No. 22 (1999)

In high school I probably got rejected seventy percent of the time. I was too skinny and too small. I ended up going to the prom by myself.

Rolling Stone (February 3, 2000)

I got rejected with my real and fake names. I didn't get discouraged, because I didn't know what it felt like to be successful. Everyone gets rejected.

Rolling Stone (February 3, 2000)

Julio Iglesias (Madrid, Spain, 1943)

Heartthrob and living legend Julio Iglesias has been one of the world's top male vocalists for the past thirty years. He won Grammys in 1987 and 1988 and is the first Latin artist to win ASCAP's Pied Piper Award.

Age bothers my legs, but not my attitude.

Variety (June 8, 1998)

Amparo Iturbi (Valencia, Spain, 1899–1969)

Raised in Spain and trained in France, Amparo Iturbi moved to the United States in 1937 and became one of the world's leading classical pianists.

[On recording sessions] The ultimate torture of the century.

Diane Telgen and Jim Kamp (eds.), *Notable Hispanic Women* (1993)

José Iturbi (Valencia, Spain, 1895–1980)

Born in Spain and trained as a pianist in France, José Iturbi moved to the United States where he and his sister Amparo had brilliant careers as soloists and in duo.

I am my sister's worst enemy.

Diane Telgen and Jim Kamp (eds.), *Notable Hispanic American Women* (1993)

J

Francisco Jiménez (San Pedro, Tlaquepaque, Mexico, 1943)

After emigrating with his family from Mexico, Francisco Jiménez worked in the fields of California. Educated at Santa Clara University and Columbia, he is currently chair of the Department of Modern Languages and Literatures and holds an endowed professorship at his alma mater. Jiménez has published and edited several books on Mexican and Mexican American literature and is the author of short stories and a book for children that have won various prizes.

> The most important step we can take toward filling the need for cultural understanding is to become well educated by the disinterested paths of art, literature, scholarship, and openhearted friendship. In the process of becoming educated we learn from each other and, in so doing, we destroy the barriers that separate us from one another; we demolish prejudices that impede us from becoming fully human.
>
> Original quotation for this book (May 2000)

> I write creatively to chronicle part of my family's history, but more importantly, to voice the experiences of a large sector of our society that has been frequently ignored. Through my writing I hope to give readers an insight into the lives of immigrant migrant farmworker families and their children whose backbreaking labor, picking fruits and vegetables, puts food on our tables. Their courage, struggles, and hopes and dreams for a better life for their children and their children's children give meaning to the term "the American Dream." Their story is the American story. In my writing I try to draw attention to and compassion for our brothers and sisters: the thousands of immigrant families and their children of yesterday and today.
>
> Original quotation for this book (May 2000)

Francisco Jiménez. Courtesy of Prof. Jiménez.

My primary goal in writing both scholarly and creative works is to fill the need for cultural and human understanding, between the United States and Mexico, in particular. I write in both English and Spanish. The language I use is determined by what period in my life I write about. Since Spanish was the dominant language during my childhood, I generally write about those experiences in Spanish. My scholarly research has been published in both English and Spanish. Because I am bilingual and bicultural, I can move in and out of both American and Mexican cultures with ease; therefore, I have been able to write stories in both languages. I consider that a privilege.

Santa Clara University Web site (March 2001)

There are many people who made this collection of short stories possible. I am indebted to my family whose lives are represented in this book. These stories are their stories as well as mine. These are also the stories of many migrant children of yesterday and today. I thank them all and ask their forgiveness for taking the liberty to write about them, knowing

full well my limitations as a writer. Their courage, tenacity, and un-
wavering hope in the midst of adversity have been a constant inspiration to me.

Francisco Jiménez, *The Circuit* (1997)

I would like to express my sincere gratitude to my teachers whose faith
in my ability and whose guidance helped me break the migrant circuit.

Francisco Jiménez, *The Circuit* (1997)

"La frontera" [the border] is a word I often heard when I was a child
living in *El Rancho Blanco,* a small village nestled on barren, dry hills
several miles north of Guadalajara, Mexico. I heard it for the first time
in the late 1940s when Papá and Mamá told me and Roberto, my older
brother, that someday we would make a long trip north, cross *la frontera,*
enter California, and leave our poverty behind.

Francisco Jiménez, *The Circuit* (1997)

Raúl Julia (San Juan, Puerto Rico, 1940–1994)

Actor Raúl Julia delighted audiences on stage and screen while supporting
the causes of Latino culture and humanitarian relief. He won two Tony
Awards, an Emmy and a Golden Globe. Two organizations, Nosotros and
La Raza, honored him for his positive portrayal of Hispanic culture and
the Hunger Project gave him the first Global Citizen Award.

Once you are willing to take responsibility for your life you become a
master of it and you expand—you become more alive and healthier,
mentally and physically.

Elle (November 1987)

You can't say one performance is better than another; it's ridiculous. It's
like saying a Chateau Lafite [wine] is better than a Chateau Latour.
Anyway, I don't measure my progress by awards.

Elle (November 1987)

A cigar is as good as the memories that you have when you smoked it.

Cigar Aficionado Web site (1998)

I have a very deep care[ing] for Latin America, and, of course, for what
was going on in El Salvador [the civil war]. I have felt outrage. I have
felt anger. And, I have felt helpless.

Cigar Aficionado Web site (1998)

Katy Jurado (Guadalajara, Mexico, 1927)

One of Hollywood's "Latin ladies," Katy Jurado played memorable roles
in the films *High Noon* (1952) and *One-Eyed Jacks* (1961) and was nominated
for an Oscar for her supporting role in *Broken Lance* (1954).

It is not one person who makes a movie, it's the actors and producers and directors who make good films. And I hope in the future that people will make good pictures for love, not money.

Acceptance speech, Golden Boot Awards (1992)

L

Richard Lacayo (New York, New York, 1952)

A freelance writer and contributor to the *New York Times*, Richard Lacayo is now a senior writer for *Time*.

> Hip was deaf to the best, blind to the truth and dressed by Penny's.
>
> *Time* (August 8, 1994)

La India (Linda Belle Caballero) (Río Piedras, Puerto Rico, 1970)

Born Linda Belle Caballero, the future singer moved as a baby to the tough La Candela section of New York City's Bronx. She began her career in hip hop and moved on to become one of the leading singers in the Nuyorican salsa movement. La India is also a songwriter.

> Women see me as a figure they can respect. They know I've been through a lot, I'm not going to let no man put me under.
>
> *Chicago Tribune* (October 31, 1997)

John Leguizamo (Bogotá, Colombia, 1964)

A rising actor and comedian, John Leguizamo has appeared in many films. In 1990 he wrote, produced and starred in his own one-man Broadway show, *Mambo Mouth* (1991), later telecasted as an HBO special. Two years later Leguizamo did another show, *Spic-O-Rama*, also taped for HBO. In 2000 he won an Emmy for the best performance in a variety or music program. Leguizamo's most recent show is *Sexaholix . . . A Love Story* (2002).

When the few good Latin parts go to non-Hispanic actors, Hollywood is saying, "You people are interesting enough to make films about, but you aren't good enough to play yourselves."

Premiere (August 1992)

Americans go through periods when they love Latin stuff. Like in the '40s, Latin was so big. Everybody was doing the samba, the cha-cha, and then we disappeared for a while. By the late '50s they were saying, "No more of you people. Latin's out." The '50s were the whitest decade.

Interview (September 1995)

I want to play the Paramount at Madison Square Garden—and do thousands of characters and elevate the Latin image in America to heights unknown. Everybody in America—black, white, Indian, Chinese—will want to be Latin.

Interview (September 1995)

Tania León (Havana, Cuba, 1943)

At the age of twenty-four, Tania León left Cuba for the United States, where she has developed her career as a composer and conductor. Her compositions express diverse musical influences from Latin America, Africa, gospel and jazz. León has conducted symphony orchestras in countries throughout the world.

It's not common for a woman of my skin color to conduct serious music, so I have to know the score inside out, or work twice as hard as male conductors.

Joseph M. Palmisano (ed.), *Notable Hispanic American Women*, Book II (1998)

Sheila Lichacz (Monagrillo, Panama, 1942)

A painter whose work has been exhibited in many countries, Sheila Lichacz was named ambassador-at-large by the president of Panama in 1995. The following year she became the first woman honored with the Hispanic Achievement Award in the category of international friendship.

The reason my work is so spiritual is that without faith, I never would have survived. None of us are going to live forever. We are all going. A nun told me when I was a freshman in college, "Make the most of yourself, because you will never happen again." That is the philosophy of my life.

Joseph M. Palmisano (ed.), *Notable Hispanic American Women*, Book II (1998)

José Limón (Culiacán, Mexico, 1908–1972)

After moving to the United States as a child, José Limón studied modern dance with Doris Humphrey and Charles Weidman. He performed in

Broadway musicals before founding his own modern dance company. Limón was the best known American choreographer and male dancer of the 1940s, 1950s and the early 1960s. Two of his works are *Lament for Ignacio Sánchez Mejías* (1947) and *La Malinche* (1949).

> Birth, for a dancer, is like this. You put on a leotard, and trembling with embarrassment and terrible shyness, you step into the studio. Humphrey, a goddess, a nymph, a caryatid, makes you do things you have never done before. You stretch; you bend and flex your legs, your arches and torso, every muscle, tendon, nerve, vein, and artery—all of you, your whole entire you. You run, jump, and turn; you fall to the floor and rise again. . . . You pant, sweat, and hurt. You learn that you are. You learn that the past—the *jarabes* [Mexican dances], the bullfights, the painting, the Mexican in you, the fearful passage to the land of the gringos, the wounds, the deaths—have been only a preparation for this new life.
>
> *Dance* (April 1999)

> In a state of pure bliss I lived (somewhat lame from muscles unaccustomed to the rigors of dance exercises) for the moment I would return to the studio.
>
> *Dance* (April 1999)

Rebecca Lobo (Hartford, Connecticut, 1973)

The only Big East basketball player to have earned simultaneously the titles of Scholar-Athlete of the Year and Player of the Year, Rebecca Lobo was an All-American center in college, the youngest member to play on the U.S. Olympic team in the 1996 Atlanta Games and one of the leading players in the fledgling WNBA. She has raised $1.4 million for cancer research and volunteers for the Children's Miracle Network.

> I enjoyed watching Dr. J. and Larry Bird play, but I looked to them as great athletes, not role models. In terms of people I wanted to be like and please, though, it was always my parents and family.
>
> *Women's Sports and Fitness* (March 1996)

Los Lobos (East Los Angeles, California, 1974)

The Chicano band Los Lobos was founded in 1974. With members David Hidalgo, Conrad Lozano, Louie Pérez and César Rojas, the group started as a rock band but soon embraced other styles, including Mexican folk music, rhythm-and-blues and punk. Los Lobos has won many awards, including Grammys, the Desi Lifetime Achievement, Rolling Stone Band of the Year and the Golden Eagle for the best film soundtrack (*La Bamba*, 1987).

David Hidalgo   A member of the band Los Lobos, David Hidalgo writes most of the group's songs.

> We never set out to make this political statement but I guess just by being there, it's a statement in itself.
>
> *Latin Music* (December 1999/January 2000)

Louie Pérez   A member of the band Los Lobos, Louie Pérez is the group's lyricist.

> This is music made by Mexican-Americans, but if you looked that up in the dictionary, I don't think you'd find our picture. We're not the kind of music people would expect, which excites me. It's nice to show that as Latinos, we can do a lot of things.
>
> *Latin Music* (December 1999/January 2000)

> We all came from the same high school. We were friends before we were ever a band. I think that's one of the reasons we've been around as long as we have.
>
> Mayan Media Web site (February 2000)

> The four of us used to hang out—we had a lot of time on our hands when we weren't rehearsing or gigging at weddings or whatnot. During the day we'd get together with a couple of acoustic guitars and we'd sit in the backyard and learn these old Mexican songs from our parents' records which we called the soundtrack of the Barrio.
>
> Mayan Media Web site (February 2000)

César Rojas   A member of the band Los Lobos, César Rojas is the group's lead guitarist and singer.

> I was put on this earth to make music. I'm proud Los Lobos got out and threw the East L.A. flag into the crowd. I'm proud that we were the only group that made it out of East L.A.
>
> *Latin Music* (December 1999/January 2000)

> Hey, it's got to be different! Who would want to make the same record over and over again? That would be so boring!
>
> Mayan Media Web site (February 2000)

> Back in the fifties, in Mexico, it could get really tough. A lot of poverty. Not only that, all the odds were against us because we were isolated, living in a little ranch with no electricity, no running water, no indoor plumbing. When you're a little kid you're just happy to be anywhere. I saw a lot of hardships, but I never connected it to anything. You sense

that there's something wrong, but you just go on being a little kid, being happy with whatever you have. Oh, they struggled so much.

Marilyn P. Davis, Mexican Voices/American Dreams (1990)

Coming to the United States—I'll never forget that! I was really afraid. This U.S., this big old monster. I was panicked. These people were speaking this other language, they dressed differently, acted differently. It's like going to another planet, you know. What intrigued me though was these other people who spoke Spanish. All these emotions were running through me. It was scary.

Marilyn P. Davis, Mexican Voices/American Dreams (1990)

There are a lot of wealthy people out there that have it all but never have had these experiences that humans need to give incentive in life, to make you feel that you've achieved something. We all need that.

Marilyn P. Davis, Mexican Voices/American Dreams (1990)

We would be rehearsing and it was like in the afternoon, and my dad would come home from work. He didn't want to hear that. The poor guy was tired from working all day. He'd come home full of grease and all burned out and we'd be blowing away the neighborhood. My dad would get really upset. He tolerated it, but he'd get pissed off. But my mom would say, "Leave him alone, leave him alone." Yeh, my dad took a lot of beatings from all over. God bless him.

Marilyn P. Davis, Mexican Voices/American Dreams (1990)

Everybody has a God-given talent. It's given to us by somebody else and it's what you do with it.

Marilyn P. Davis, Mexican Voices/American Dreams (1990)

It's been a struggle, but it's been more fun than anything else. I used to think that this must be a crime, there must be a law against having so much fun and being successful. But then I think that no, I was destined to do this, so here I am and I give it my best.

Marilyn P. Davis, Mexican Voices/American Dreams (1990)

Barry López (Port Chester, New York, 1945)

Writer and ecologist Barry López has published many books and essays on nature and other subjects.

As one grew older, he said, one learned that with enough care almost anything would keep. It was only a matter of choosing what to take care of.

Barry López, Winter Count (1981)

The land is like poetry; it is inexplicably coherent, it is transcendent in its meaning, and it has the power to elevate a consideration of human life.

Barry López, *Artic Dreams* (1986)

The perceptions of many people wash over the land like a flood, leaving ideas hung up in the brush, like pieces of damp paper to be collected and deciphered. No one can tell the whole story.

Arctic Dreams (1986)

The moral dimension of language must be brought out. All good writers are troublemakers, all good writers are sworn enemies of complacency and dogma.

Introduction, Stephen Trimble, *Words from the Land* (1988)

Felipe López (Santo Domingo, Dominican Republic, 1974)

After a brilliant college career at St. John's University in New York, shooting guard Felipe López joined the Vancouver Grizzlies professional basketball team. His family is from the Dominican Republic.

Whatever I do on the court is *para mi gente* [for my people].

Latina (October 1998)

It makes me proud to be from *una cultura tan preciosa* [such a beautiful culture] and to break down walls for Latino kids.

Latina (October 1998)

Jennifer López (Bronx, New York, 1970)

Actress and singer Jennifer López is well known for her portrayal of Selena, the murdered Tejano singer, in the movie *Selena* (1997). She was nominated for a Golden Globe as best actress for this role. She has appeared in *U-Turn* (1997), *Out of Sight* (1998), *Thieves* (1999), *The Cell* (2000), *Angel Eyes* (2001) and *Maid in Manhattan* (2002).

I always knew I wanted to be a performer, and my mother started taking me to dance classes when I was five. My mother is a teacher, my father works at an insurance company. When I said I wanted to be a performer, people went, "Yeah, right." You don't do that where I come from.

Interview (April 1997)

Being Latino in this country, we're all looked at the same. They don't look at us and go, "She's Salvadoran," or, "She's Puerto Rican."

Interview (April 1997)

Jennifer López. Photo by Rafy. Courtesy of Photofest.

My life has always been a wonderful life, but it's a big life, and you get big problems. It's always a struggle.

Teen People (May 2000)

Josefina López (Cerritos, San Luis Potosí, Mexico, 1969)

Josefina María López published her first play when she was seventeen years old. The work won a Gold Award from the Corporation for Public Broadcasting. López has also worked as a screenwriter and a producer for television.

I've taken our beautiful hot and fiery colors of Mexico and mixed them with American feminism and freedom of speech.

Los Angeles Times (July 29, 1990)

Lourdes López (Havana, Cuba, 1958)

Lourdes López became a principal dancer for the New York City Ballet while juggling the roles of wife, mother and student, a rare combination for prima ballerinas. She has danced in solo and company tours in England, France, Denmark, Germany and China. She retired from the New York City Ballet in 1997.

> My mother's always been there with me. She's not pushy like a stage mother. It's just that she said, "If you want to be a dancer, I'm behind you all the way."
>
> *Miami Herald* (October 3, 1975)

Luis López (Cidra, Puerto Rico, 1970)

One of the most versatile athletes in major league baseball, Luis López can play shortstop, second or third base. "Papi" comes from a family of baseball players.

> *Hay tantos peloteros superestrellas* [There are so many superstars in baseball], I'm just lucky to be doing what I love.
>
> *Latina* (October 1998)

> My family always comes first.
>
> *Latina* (October 1998)

> [Regarding his wife] It's really hard, but I try to be *detallista* (thoughtful). I send her flowers, take her out dancing when I'm home.
>
> *Latina* (October 1998)

Nancy López (Torrance, California, 1957)

Remembered for her unmatched record of nine tournament wins (five in a row) in her rookie season, Nancy López is a member of both the LPGA Hall of Fame and the PGA World Golf Hall of Fame. She received the 1998 Bob Jones Award for sportsmanship, one of the highest honors in her sport. López has won more than 130 tournaments in her career. Her large, vociferous group of fans is sometimes known as "Nancy's Navy."

> When I'm here [at home] . . . taking care of my family, I don't even know who wins the tournaments. . . . I *enjoy* my other life—being a mom and being home.
>
> *Southern Living* (October 1999)

> I've always taught my kids to be their best, and you have to set your highest goal because if you don't, you're never going to be better.
>
> *Southern Living* (October 1999)

Yolanda López (San Diego, California, 1942)

Known especially for her striking portraits of the Virgin of Guadalupe, Yolanda López is a painter, professor and women's rights activist.

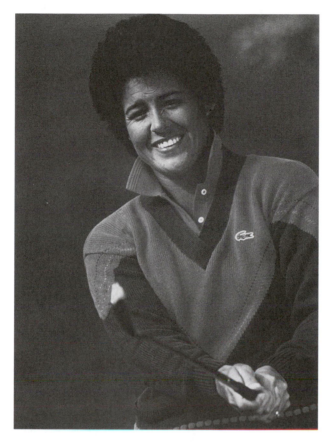

Nancy López. Courtesy of International Management Group.

In the first grade there was a chalkboard, and, while the boys drew airplanes and bombs, I did little farm animals with straw hats.

Betty LaDuke, *Women Artists: Multi-Cultural Visions* (1992)

The streets were my gallery. I saw my work everywhere, and unsigned.

Betty LaDuke, *Women Artists: Multi-Cultural Visions* (1992)

Endurance is one of our greatest survival skills.

Feminist Studies (Spring 1994)

M

Eduardo Machado (Havana, Cuba, 1953)

The author of more than twenty-five plays, Eduardo Machado is also a movie and television director. He has taught theater at Columbia University.

> "Hispanic" covers a wide range of theatrical, political and social ideas—as diverse and colorful as America itself.
>
> *Plays from South Coast Repertory: Hispanic Playwrights Project Anthology* (2000)

Alberto Manguel (Buenos Aires, Argentina, 1948)

Novelist, editor and critic Alberto Manguel has worked in Italy, France, England and Canada. He has written numerous books including *News from a Foreign Country Came* (1991), winner of the McKitterick Prize for best novel, and *A History of Reading* (1996).

> Old favorites are often sacred cows grown tough with age.
>
> *New York Times* (August 23, 1987)

> Because reading is a lonely vice, we frequently bring others into our reading . . . nudge them to listen, share our delight or disgust, judge our selection. Every reader is an anthologist who breeds readers.
>
> *New York Times* (August 23, 1987)

Sonia Manzano (New York, New York, 1950)

Actress and writer for the famous television program *Sesame Street*, Sonia Manzano has played the role of María, the show's leading Hispanic character. She has earned several Emmy Awards and been recognized for her work by the Hispanic Congressional Caucus in Washington, D.C.

That's why I love being on "Sesame Street" so much. I'm happy to be in a situation where I'm not asked to be like anyone else.

Diane Telgen and Jim Kamp (eds.), *Notable Hispanic American Women* (1993)

Constance Marie (East Los Angeles, California, 1969)

Constance Marie (López) has been an actress in film and television. She played an important role in Gregory Nava's movie *My Family* (1995).

[On being a Latina actress] Once you're in, you not only have to be better than everyone else but you have to rise above your best and be brilliant because of how we are perceived.

Moderna (Fall 1997)

An actor has to have the hide of a rhinoceros and the soul of a rose.

Moderna (Fall 1997)

Richard "Cheech" Marín (Los Angeles, California, 1946)

Comic, actor and writer, Richard Marín launched his career in the comedy team of Cheech and Chong. After the duo's split, he continued his career as an actor, screenwriter and director.

See, my [nick]name came about when an uncle saw me in the crib. He said, "This baby *parece un chicharrón* (looks like pork cracklings)! The name stuck.

Latina (March 2001)

I never ditched school. I did go cruising in lowriders, and I always got straight A's.

Latina (March 2001)

I find things about me on our Web site that I've never done. The other day I looked and it said I'd done a version of the "Macarena" and called it "Gonorrhea."

Latina (March 2001)

Patricia Preciado Martín (Tuscon, Arizona, 1939)

Patricia Preciado Martín served in the Peace Corps, taught junior and senior high school and is an author who has attempted to preserve the oral heritage of the Mexican American people.

I think it's very important that Mexican Americans feel a sense of place because we're always told to go back from where we came.

Joseph M. Palmisano (ed.), *Notable Hispanic American Women*, Book II (1998)

Ricky Martín (San Juan, Puerto Rico, 1971)

Former member of the teen rock group Menudo, Ricky Martín became a music sensation in 1999 with the number 1 song in America, "Livin' la Vida Loca." He is the most popular example of crossover and fusion, a musical style that combines Latin and pop influences. Martín also co-starred in the musical *Les Misérables* on Broadway and has appeared in the ABC soap opera *General Hospital*.

> [On crossover music] It was very important for me to do this kind of music because it helps me to break boundaries. That's what I want, that's what I need to do. I feel the need to do it because, I'm very lucky, I'm in a career that makes it very easy for me to go to different countries because it's about music. I have to, I want to, keep doing these kind of rhythms, hey, I'm *Latin*, I get the swing of it.
>
> Interview with Little Judy, *LaMusica* Web site (1996)

> The feeling that I get when I'm on stage . . . I will never change that for anything. It gives you strength, it gives you some kind of power, it gives

Ricky Martín. Courtesy of Photofest.

you control. What do I want to be doing in thirty years? I want to do this; I want to do music. Let's keep studying, let's keep getting ready.

Interview with Little Judy, *LaMusica* Web site (1996)

It's all about breaking stereotypes. For me, the fact that people think Puerto Rico is "Scarface" [the gangster movie], that we ride donkeys to school—that has to change.

Entertainment Weekly (April 23, 1999)

My music is freedom. It hits the nail on the head.

Rolling Stone (August 5, 1999)

Instead of [my] grabbing America by storm, America caught me. Ever since, I've been living, literally, la vida loca—the crazy life.

"Ricky Revolution," *Rolling Stone* Web site (1999)

The way we humans are living life right now, we are living half of it. A lot of people tell me I am negative if I see it that way but I think I am realistic. . . . If I have the chance to send a message in my songs, why not. . . . It is a "Hello. . . . Wake up!"

"Ricky Revolution," *Rolling Stone* Web site (1999)

Julie A. Martines (Winfield, Illinois, 1966)

A career businesswoman, Julie A. Martines is also active in Hispanic American and other service organizations.

You have to prove yourself—you have to do that every day in business. But because of gender or race, some of us have to do it a little more.

Latina (August 1997)

I love working for myself. I have never worked so hard in my life, but the results are well worth it! I encourage women of any age to do whatever they can to establish themselves, learn skills, and gain independence so they can be financially and personally rewarded through their own achievements.

Hispanic (August 31, 1995)

Elizabeth Martínez (Pomona, California, 1943)

After her university studies, Elizabeth Martínez joined the Los Angeles County Public Library as California's first Mexican American librarian. She later became librarian for the Orange County Public Library, city librarian for the Los Angeles Public Library and executive director of the American Library Association. Martínez also lectures and has her own consulting firm.

Books were a kind of escape. I visited places I'd never seen.

> Joseph M. Palmisano (ed.), *Notable Hispanic American Women*, Book II (1998)

Pedro Martínez (Manoguayabo, Dominican Republic, 1971)

By the time he was twenty-nine, Pedro "Tino" Martínez had already won two Cy Young Awards, one in the American League and one in the National League.

I play this game because I love it, ever since I played in the street with a ball of string.

> *Kansas City Star* (March 24, 2000)

I hate signing action pictures. That is one ugly face.

> *Sports Illustrated* (March 27, 2000)

I am a pitcher because I like the challenge of being responsible for the game, of being in charge of the action.

> *Sports Illustrated* (March 27, 2000)

I watch and learn.

> *Sports Illustrated* (March 27, 2000)

I'm not afraid of hitting anyone, because I can put the ball where I want to. . . . When I do hit them, it's usually just a nibble. I can nibble their jersey with the ball. That's how much I can control the ball.

> *Sports Illustrated* (March 27, 2000)

I will do my best. It will be hard to do. But I tell you, I will try every time out.

> *Sports Illustrated* (March 27, 2000)

What do I mean when I say I pitch from my heart? It means something inside me—a feeling I get. It's in my blood, my body. It's not the money. The money, it never steps inside the white lines. It's my pride, my name. My family's name. My reputation.

> *Current Biography* (June 2001)

Rubén Martínez (1962)

Rubén Martínez is a journalist and poet. Raised in Los Angeles, he considers this city to be the best example of the new hybrid culture in the United States.

We were an American family, assimilated, middle-class. We spoke English, except for my mother's terms of endearment like *m'hijo* (my son).

And there was her heavy accent, which my brother, sister, and I made fun of.

"The Shock of the New," Antonia Darder and Rodolfo D. Torres (eds.), *The Latino Studies Reader* (1998)

My Mexican grandparents were mysterious figures from far-off lands, their voices even thicker with the accent of another time and place. They could only half understand their grandchildren. Isolated in their world, they waited for death while living in memory, satisfied that they'd done the right thing by ensuring their children and grandchildren a better life in the United States.

"The Shock of the New," Antonia Darder and Rodolfo D. Torres (eds.), *The Latino Studies Reader* (1998)

We are not in Mexico, nor in Aztlán, the mythical Chicano nation separate from white America. But we're not quite in the United States, either. We're in Los Angeles.

"The Shock of the New," Antonia Darder and Rodolfo D. Torres (eds.), *The Latino Studies Reader* (1998)

I have . . . dreamed of a California in which a historical wound hundreds of years old might be healed: a reconciliation between North and South, the Catholic and the Protestant, the First and Third Worlds. I've come to admit that rock'n'roll is as important to my spiritual well-being as *la Virgen de Guadalupe*. I will always be the outsider in Latin America. I also oftentimes feel like an outcast in the United States. The only place I could be at home is in the new—the almost new—Los Angeles.

"The Shock of the New," Antonia Darder and Rodolfo D. Torres (eds.), *The Latino Studies Reader* (1998)

For the new generation [of Chicanos], activism and Aztlán, the mythical Chicano land of milk and honey, separate from white America, are viable again.

"The Shock of the New," Antonia Darder and Rodolfo D. Torres (eds.), *The Latino Studies Reader* (1998)

Silvia A. Martínez (Unknown place and date of birth)

Silvia A. Martínez is acting editor-in-chief of *Latina* magazine.

On Mother's Day in many Latin American countries, people wear a rosebud—red if your mom is alive, white if she has passed away—on their lapel. It's a public display of love, a small offering to honor that special woman, wherever she may be.

Latina (May 2000)

Milagros Mateu (New York, New York, 1947)

Milagros "Millie" Mateu has worked in bilingual education. She runs the Hispanic education program at NASA.

> Do something you truly love doing, something you can truly believe in. And be the best you can be at it.
>
> Joseph M. Palmisano (ed.), *Notable Hispanic American Women*, Book II (1998)

Nicholasa Mohr (New York, New York, 1935)

A writer whose works have undone the view of Spanish Harlem as a masculine place of violence, drugs and gangs, Nicholasa Mohr has won several prizes, including the New York Times Outstanding Book of the Year, the *School Library Journal* Best Children's Book. She holds an honorary degree from the New York State legislature. Mohr was the first Hispanic woman in the United States to develop a career as a creative writer for major publishing houses. She is also a painter.

> Hispanic literature is a vital and important aspect of contemporary American society, and it is not being read because it is not being published! The best way to censor a people is to ignore them. In this way there is not even the possibility of confrontation. And, those enjoying such eminence and affluence need have no fear that the literature of the people of color will in any way impinge or threaten their well-guarded empire.
>
> *Americas Review* (Fall/Winter 1986)

Gloria Molina (Los Angeles, California, 1948)

Political activist, politician and administrator Gloria Molina was the first Mexican American woman to be elected to the Assembly of the California legislature, the Los Angeles City Council and the Los Angeles County Board of Supervisors. She was founding president of the Comisión Femenil de Los Ángeles and cofounder of the Centro de Niños. She has been named Woman of the Year by the Mexican American Opportunity Foundation and *Ms.* magazine and received the Aztec Eagle Award, the highest honor given to a foreigner by the government of Mexico.

> Latinos have made many advancements in just my lifetime alone. More of us are going to college, buying homes, and entering into the middle class. However, much needs to be done and it is up to each one of us to do our best—to stay in school, work hard, and become productive members of our communities. Only then can we realize the goal that all Americans have an equal chance to share in the American Dream.
>
> Original quotation for this book (December 2000)

Los Angeles County Supervisor Gloria Molina. Courtesy
of Ms. Molina.

María Móntez (Ciudad Trujillo, Dominican Republic, 1920–1951)

The daughter of the Spanish consul to the Dominican Republic, actress
María África Gracis Vidal de Santos Silas changed her name to María
Móntez when she signed a contract with Universal Pictures. She per-
formed in many exotic roles before her early death.

I am here to tempt the hearts of men.
> Line from *Ali Baba and the Forty Thieves* (1944)

Out of fifteen pictures, in about thirteen either I have been in a bath or
a swim[ming pool].
> *Saturday Evening Post* (June 28, 1945)

[On acting in westerns] Every time I begin to emote, I look up and there
is a horse—stealing my scene.
> *Saturday Evening Post* (June 28, 1945)

José Montoya (El Gallego, New Mexico, 1932)

The son of a migrant laborer, poet José Montoya was raised in New Mexico and California. He has published several books.

Oppression has kept us razor sharp.
Wolfgang Binder (ed.), *Partial Autobiographies: Interviews with Twenty Chicano Poets* (1985)

Joseph M. Montoya (Penablanca, New Mexico, 1915–1978)

United States congressman and senator Joseph Manuel Montoya began his political career as the youngest representative ever elected to the New Mexico House of Representatives. Later he would be a member of the state's Senate, lieutenant governor of New Mexico and U.S. representative and senator (Democrat). He worked on behalf of civil rights, education and health care.

[Against violence in politics] We have watched carefully as others pounded upon portals of American life with gun butts and clenched

Senator Joseph M. Montoya. Courtesy of the Center for Southwest Research, General Library, University of New Mexico.

fists. This has been their choice. I put such an option aside and decry negativism.

Charles Moritz (ed.), *Current Biography Yearbook* (1975)

We must find a way to renew the revolution in the hearts and minds of people.

Maurilio E. Vigil, *Hispanics in Congress* (1996)

I know that we still have not convinced the majority of Americans of the value of bilingualism or the multicultural society. But I know, too, that more and more Americans every day understand that in a world which is multicultural and multilingual, our nation is strengthened and enriched every time we expand our own multicultural traditions.

Maurilio E. Vigil, *Hispanics in Congress* (1996)

Of all the nations in the world, ours should have the greatest ability to appreciate cultural and linguistic variety.

Maurilio E. Vigil, *Hispanics in Congress* (1996)

Linda L. Montoya (Santa Fe, New Mexico, 1947)

Linda L. Montoya is a photographer whose work has been exhibited in the United States and Germany. She has also worked in cinema.

For me, going to Mexico was like finding my roots.

Impact: Albuquerque Journal Magazine (November 20, 1984)

The only way I can do my portraits is to know my subjects. Anytime I've done it without knowing them, I've felt that I was intruding on their souls.

Impact: Albuquerque Journal Magazine (November 20, 1984)

Growing up in Santa Fe, New Mexico, as a Hispanic, I never experienced being from a minority group. The Hispanic population was considered the majority. When I got married and moved away to Massachusetts . . . for the first time I experienced cultural shock, I felt like a fish out of water. When I discovered photography, I used my camera to document my life journey. Reflections of the world around me, through the use of my camera, have given me a place of belonging and I no longer feel like a fish out of water.

Original quotation for this book (July 2001)

Antonio Mora (Havana, Cuba)

Born in Cuba, raised in Venezuela and now a resident of the United States, Antonio Mora is the only Latino anchor for a national news program on Hispanic television. He reports the news on *Good Morning America*.

Linda Montoya. Photo by Catherine Martínez. Courtesy of Ms. Montoya and LM Images.

I feel a very large responsibility as a representative of the Hispanic community.

Cristina (October 2000)

[I am somebody] who gets along with everyone. I like people and I am not a complicated person.

Cristina (October 2000)

I don't fear old age; I live waiting for it.

Cristina (October 2000)

Pat Mora (El Paso, Texas, 1942)

A Latina educator, poet and essayist who writes about life on the border, Pat Mora began her career in literature at the age of forty. She has also been a radio commentator and a museum director. Mora has received the New America Award for her poetry and the Harvey L. Johnson Book

Award from the Southwest Council of Latin American Studies. Her work has been translated into Spanish, Italian and Bengali.

> I revel in a certain Mexican passion not for life or about life, but *in* life, a certain intensity in the daily living of it, a certain abandon in . . . music, in the hugs, sometimes in the anger.
>
> *Christian Science Monitor* (July 19, 1990)

> When I hear a phrase in Spanish in a Cincinnati restaurant, my head turns quickly. I listen, silently wishing to be part of that other conversation—if only for a few moments, to feel Spanish in my mouth.
>
> *Christian Science Monitor* (July 19, 1990)

> [Advertisements] convince us that our cars, clothes, and even families aren't good enough . . . being beautiful is being thin, blond, and rich, rich, rich.
>
> *Horn Book* (July/August 1990)

> I write to try to correct these images of worth. I take pride in being a Hispanic writer. I will continue to write and to struggle to say what no other writer can say in quite the same way.
>
> *Horn Book* (July/August 1990)

> Language like light can seep into us. Language too heals.
>
> Pat Mora Web site (April 2000)

> Together may we protect the world's beauty including its peoples, their cultures and languages. Light, language, laughter: all are powerful. May we laugh often together.
>
> Pat Mora Web site (April 2000)

Cherríe Moraga (Whittier, California, 1952)

Poet, playwright, essayist and editor, Cherríe Moraga is a founder of Kitchen Table: Women of Color Press. She has won fellowships from the National Endowment for the Arts and the Fund for New American Plays. Moraga has taught at the University of California, Berkeley.

> I am a very tired Chicana/half-breed/feminist/lesbian/writer/teacher/talker/waitress. And I am not alone in this.
>
> Cherríe Moraga and Gloria Anzaldua (eds.), *This Bridge Called My Back: Writings by Radical Women of Color* (1981)

> The revolution begins at home.
>
> Cherríe Moraga and Gloria Anzaldua (eds.), *This Bridge Called My Back: Writings by Radical Women of Color* (1981)

I am afraid to get near to how deeply I want the love of other Latin women in my life.

>Cherríe Moraga and Gloria Anzaldua (eds.), *This Bridge Called My Back: Writings by Radical Women of Color* (1981)

The only thing worth writing about is what seems to be unknown and, therefore, fearful.

>Cherríe Moraga and Gloria Anzaldua (eds.), *This Bridge Called My Back: Writings by Radical Women of Color* (1981)

I am a Chicana lesbian . . . in direct contradiction to, and in violation of, the women I was raised to be.

>Cherríe Moraga and others, *Loving in the War Years* (1983)

Family is *not* by definition the man in the dominant position over women and children. *Familia* is cross-generational bonding, deep emotional ties between opposite sexes, and within our sex. It is sexuality which . . . springs forth from touch, constant and daily.

>Cherríe Moraga and others, *Loving in the War Years* (1983)

Spirituality which inspires activism and, similarly, politics which move the spirit—which draw from the deep-seated place of our greatest longings for freedom—give meaning to our lives.

>Cherríe Moraga and others, *Loving in the War Years* (1983)

Jonathan D. Moreno (Poughkeepsie, New York, 1952)

A staff member of former President Clinton's Advisory Committee on Human Radiation Experiments, Jonathan D. Moreno is Kornfeld Professor of Biomedical Ethics and Director of the Center for Biomedical Ethics at the University of Virginia. He is a regular contributor on bioethics to ABC News Web site.

[To medical students working on cadavers] We require you to be the agents of a disintegration of a human body far more systematic and bloodless than that of the field of battle.

>*New York Times* (February 23, 1991)

Rita Moreno (Rosa Dolores Alverio) (Humacao, Puerto Rico, 1931)

Actress, singer and dancer, Rita Moreno is the only female performer who has won all four of the most prestigious awards in show business—the Oscar, Emmy, Tony and Grammy.

It's tough getting roles being a woman, but being both female and Puerto Rican makes it all that much harder. I think the barriers, the stereotypes, actually are finally falling apart.

San Francisco Chronicle (September 14, 1976)

I want to show that I can play several kinds of roles, not just Latinas, though I look forward to good Latina parts.

San Francisco Chronicle (September 14, 1976)

Like many aspiring actresses, I came to Hollywood wanting nothing more than to be the next Lana Turner, but my education was to be abrupt and painful: the doors of opportunity were only open to me on strict conditions which the studios dictated. Like hundreds of other ethnic actors, I was relegated to playing a spate of nameless Indian maidens and Mexican spitfires. . . . We played the roles we were given no matter how demeaning they might have been.

Luis Reyes and Peter Rubie, *Hispanics in Hollywood* (1994)

After winning an Academy Award for playing Anita in *West Side Story* I spent years turning down roles that were veiled versions of the same role, but without the substance that *West Side Story* possessed. Thus, I turned to theater to practice my craft. I did everything in my power to seek out venues that were less inclined to typecasting.

Luis Reyes and Peter Rubie, *Hispanics in Hollywood* (1994)

Too long has it taken the entertainment industry to embrace the scope of Latino talent. Nevertheless, throughout the years Latino actors have made many significant contributions to film and television and will undoubtedly continue to do so.

Luis Reyes and Peter Rubie, *Hispanics in Hollywood* (1994)

I choose music that makes me happy. I don't in any sense pander to the popular taste, unless I happen to like it.

California State University Web site (November 1996)

Manny Mota (Santo Domingo, Dominican Republic, 1938)

The all-time record holder for the number of pinch-hits in the major leagues, Manuel Rafael Gerónimo Mota stayed with the Los Angeles Dodgers for over thiry years and appeared in three World Series. He spent fourteen years as a player before becoming a coach in 1982. He founded the Manny Mota Foundation, which feeds hundreds of children daily and conducts toy and food drives for needy families in Los Angeles and the Dominican Republic.

[Referring to the fans in the outfield of Dodger Stadium] I'm the only representative of Latin America and it's a great honor to be alongside such great company who have given so much to the game of baseball. I'm very proud to be Latino and represent my country.

Latin Style (September 1999)

I try to give good advice whenever I can so that the kids can grow up to be good fathers, good sons, and good citizens. We want their families to be proud of them.

Latin Style (September 1999)

Cecilia Muñoz (Detroit, Michigan, 1962)

A leader in immigration and civil rights policy, Cecilia Muñoz won a coveted MacArthur Foundation Grant in 2000.

We [Latinas] are very susceptible to what others think about us, so we absorb those negative stereotypes in defiance of the facts.

Washington Post (October 10, 1995)

N

Gregory Nava (San Diego, California, 1949)

Writer, producer and director Gregory Nava achieved his first success with the film *El Norte* (1983). His other movies include *My Family* (1994) and *Selena* (1996). He coproduced, wrote and directed *American Family*, the PBS series about Mexican American life in East Los Angeles.

> Even though I'm a third generation native Californian, some of my immediate relatives, who live just a few miles from the house I was raised in, are Mexican. So I've always been raised in that border world, with that tremendous clash between the cultures.
>
> *Cineáste* (Fall 1995)

> We are a nation of immigrants, and the process of immigration is very interesting to me. I come from an immigrant family, and therefore I find that the problems that immigrants have—the problems of acceptance and assimilation in a country that is based on its diversity and yet the central mainstream of which is Anglo—are all the things of great drama and great conflict. So it is my own experience which inspires me to tell these stories.
>
> *Cineáste* (Fall 1995)

> I think that ultimately Latino culture is a life-affirming culture, and despite all the tragedy and discrimination and injustice, that people endure.
>
> *Cineáste* (Fall 1995)

> I think the creative process is a very complex one in which you try to see things that are universal about family experiences and stories, the threads that run through these families, so that you can capture that

reality. . . . It kind of all goes in there and then, like a dream, it all comes back out, and I think the less you analyze it, the better.

Cineáste (Fall 1995)

Sonia M. Nieto (Brooklyn, New York, 1943)

The daughter of Puerto Rican immigrants, Sonia M. Nieto has worked and published books in the fields of bilingual and multicultural education.

For me, ethnicity means my language and it means my languages. And how I combine my languages, and how I express myself. And it's a primary part of my identity, but it's only a part. It means my birth family, and my home, and my childhood memories, and the senses and smells of my past and also of my present.

Harvard Educational Review (Spring 1994)

Antonia Novello (Fajardo, Puerto Rico, 1944)

When former President George Bush named Antonia Flores Novello as Surgeon General of the United States in 1989, she was the first woman and the first Hispanic to become the nation's highest medical officer. An early victim of chronic colon disease, she decided to study medicine and dedicate herself to alleviating suffering in children. As surgeon general, Novello concentrated on the fight against pediatric AIDS; as UNICEF's special representative for health and nutrition, she focused on smoking and drug abuse among teenagers. She has received numerous awards and honorary degrees.

You become a true caring physician when you're able to share the pain.

Glamour (August 1990)

I do believe that some people fall through the cracks. I was one of these.

Saturday Evening Post (May/June 1991)

I survived many times in my life by learning to laugh at myself.

Saturday Evening Post (May/June 1991)

In years past, RJ Reynolds [leading tobacco company] would have us walk a mile for a Camel. Today, it's time that we invite Joe Camel himself to take a hike.

New York Times (March 10, 1992)

[At her swearing-in ceremony in the White House] The American dream is alive and well today. I might say today that the *West Side Story* comes to the West Wing.

Current Biography (May 1992)

Life issues you a card, and you have to learn to play it.

Current Biography (May 1992)

O

Adriana C. Ocampo (Barranquilla, Colombia, 1955)

Born in Colombia and raised in Argentina and the United States, Adriana C. Ocampo is a planetary geologist who has worked on NASA missions to Mars and Jupiter. She is a member of the Chicxulub Consortium, an organization that studies an important meteor crater in the Yucatan Peninsula. Ocampo has been an officer in the Society of Hispanic Engineers.

> Space exploration holds the secret to the evolution of our planet and the origin of life on earth. It is part of the future of human beings.
>
> Diane Telgen and Jim Kamp (eds.), *Notable Hispanic American Women* (1993)

Ellen Ochoa (Los Angeles, California, 1958)

When she blasted off in the space shuttle *Discovery* in 1993, Ellen Ochoa became the first Latina astronaut. A veteran of three rocket flights, she has logged over 700 hours in space. Ochoa holds a doctorate in electrical engineering from Stanford University and is a mother, a classical flutist and a private pilot.

> If you stay in school, you have the potential to achieve what you want in the future.
>
> *Hispanic* (May 1990)

> Being a role model was certainly not my original intent for wanting to be an astronaut, but it's an added benefit.
>
> *Latina* (May 1998)

Edward James Olmos (East Los Angeles, California, 1947)

Actor, producer, director and community activist, Edward James Olmos speaks an average of 150 times a year at schools, charities and juvenile

Edward James Olmos. Courtesy of Arte Público Press.

institutions throughout the United States. His film credits include *Zoot Suit* (1981), *Stand and Deliver* (1988) and *Selena* (1996); more recently he has starred in *American Family*, the PBS dramatic series set in East Los Angeles.

> This film about our people *[Stand and Deliver]* will touch the nation. It shows we can achieve anything we want. Being able to make a film like this is the finest moment of my life.
>
> *Los Angeles Times* (March 27, 1988)

> We were all poor. And the only way to survive it was through a constant struggle of trying to be better today than you were yesterday.
>
> *Parade* (March 17, 1991)

> A segment of our nation's youth is growing up in a self-perpetuating lifestyle spent in and out of prison, resulting in violent crime, drugs, and certain death.
>
> Luis Reyes and Peter Rubie, *Hispanics in Hollywood* (1994)

The key to my success has been to discipline myself to do the things I don't like to do so that I'll have the discipline to do the things I like when I don't want to do them. That makes you very strong and also gives you a tremendous sense of self-worth because you're doing things for yourself.

Latinos (February/March 1997)

What makes this country strong is not economic might. No. What makes it strong is that all these beautiful, wonderful cultures live here. And what are we doing? Heading into the twenty-first century with English only.

San Francisco Examiner (April 16, 1999)

We are so "not in tune" with cultural diversity . . . that you're going to consider me a racist for the next statement I make: This country still believes, still believes, that Jesus Christ had blond hair and blue eyes.

San Francisco Examiner (April 19, 1999)

I believe that diversity is the single most unifying factor on the planet.

Bakersfield Californian (September 15, 1999)

Politically speaking, *americanos* is one of the most encompassing words in this Western Hemisphere. *Todos somos americanos* [we are all Americans].

El Andar (Winter 1999)

The beauty of the Latino experience is that we are Caucasian, that we are African, that we are Asian, we are indigenous and that we are *mezclados* [mixed]. That's the beauty of all races, and yet we do not celebrate.

El Andar (Winter 1999)

Too often society sees us not as Americans but as strangers to this land. We have worked hard to help build this country and we continue to do so every day. The face of America should include us.

Edward James Olmos, Lea Ybarra and Manuel Monterrey, *Americanos: Latino Life in the United States* (1999)

As Latinos we often think of *Americanos* as the others in this country, not us. We, and especially our children, need to see that we are an integral part of U.S. society.

Edward James Olmos, Lea Ibarra and Manuel Monterrey, *Americanos: Latino Life in the United States* (1999)

Katherine D. Ortega (Tularosa, New Mexico, 1934)

The first woman to become president of a commercial bank in California, Katherine Dávalos Ortega served as treasurer of the United States from 1983 to 1989. She has received many honorary degrees.

In the next year or so, my signature will appear on $60 billion of United States currency. More important to me, however, is the signature that appears on my life—the strong, proud, assertive handwriting of a loving father and mother.

Time (August 19, 1984)

Dyana Ortelli (Unknown place and date of birth)

Although she likes to conceal her place and date of birth, comedienne Dyana Ortelli does not hide her Mexican background. She belongs to a musical group called Hot and Spicy Mamas and has acted in films such as *Three Amigos* (1986), *Born in East L.A.* (1987) and *La Bamba* (1987).

The images we see of our people are frightening—they are criminals, maids, and prostitutes. Hispanics don't get cast as doctors and lawyers. We never get to play a significant and dignified role in our culture.

Daily Variety (August 18, 1992)

P

Américo Paredes (Brownsville, Texas, 1915)

A seminal Mexican American scholar, Américo Paredes trained a whole school of folklorists in the American Southwest. He published many studies of *corridos* (ballads), folktales and folksongs. In 1990 the government of Mexico honored Paredes with the Águila Azteca, its highest award for a foreign citizen.

> [Hispanic] legends are ego-supporting devices. They may appeal to the group or to individuals by affording them pride, dignity and self-esteem: local or national heroes to identify with, for example, or place-name legends giving an aura of importance to some familiar and undistinguished feature of the local landscape. . . . Legends . . . are important in providing symbols that embody the social aspirations of the group, whether these be embodied in an ideal status quo or in dreams of revolution.
>
> Wayland D. Hand (ed.), *American Folk Legend: A Symposium* (1971)

Yanira Paz (Maracaibo, Venezuela, 1954)

While teaching at several American universities, Yanira Paz has published two collections of poetry and several articles on Spanish linguistics and Latin American literature.

> The values that North America is selling abroad are not the values of its wonderful literature nor its art in general, but the values of McDonald's and Mickey Mouse—in other words, the free market. The free market and literature are not always good allies.
>
> *anq (American Notes & Queries)* (Summer 1997)

I would like very much to see what Hispanic culture and the Spanish language are going to be twenty years from now in the United States. Some people have stated that this is a "silent" reconquest. There is nothing silent about us.

Original quotation for this book (September 2001)

Carlos Peña (Santo Domingo, Dominican Republic, 1978)

Born and raised in the Dominican Republic, baseball player Carlos Peña moved to the United States at the age of fifteen, became an engineering student in college and a first-round draft pick by the Texas Rangers.

Except for the Native American Indians, we all came here for the same reason. . . . From the Pilgrims on, we've come here looking for the same dream, and we've all found that it's a heckuva lot tougher than we thought it would be. Which means we all have had to work a lot harder. That's all.

Cigar Aficionado (April 2000)

Elizabeth Peña (Elizabeth, New Jersey, 1959)

An actress in both film and television, Elizabeth Peña costarred with Rubén Blades in *Crossover Dreams* (1985) and played in Luis Valdez's *La Bamba* (1987). In 1988 she received a Congressional Award and was named Woman of the Year by the Hispanic Women's Council.

There's a whole new breed. . . . They are just well-trained actors who just happen to be Hispanic. We're just playing people and not playing the results of people, especially negative people.

Los Angeles Herald Examiner (July 6, 1987)

Federico F. Peña (Laredo, Texas, 1947)

The first Latino to be elected mayor of a city without a large Hispanic population (Denver, Colorado), Federico F. Peña was named secretary of transportation and secretary of energy by former President Bill Clinton. He has also been a state congressman from Colorado, a staff lawyer for the Mexican-American Legal Defense and Educational Fund and a legal advisor for the Chicano Education Project.

It's taken me time to understand there will always be someone who opposes me. I have had to learn to be a little more thick-skinned, yet not become an insensitive armadillo.

Rocky Mountain News (August 6, 1989)

My parents, in very subtle ways, instilled in us the desire to be the best, although they were never disappointed if we fell short.

Current Biography (October 1993)

Hilda Perera (Havana, Cuba, 1926)

One of the most prolific and well-known authors of children's literature in the Spanish-speaking world, Hilda Perera has won Spain's prestigious Lazarillo Award (equivalent to the Newberry Award) and the Hispanic Heritage Award. She has lived in the United States since 1964.

> I had two children and they started asking me for stories, so I started making stories for them. That was the beginning.
>
> Joseph M. Palmisano (ed.), *Notable Hispanic American Women*, Book II (1998)

Rosie Pérez (Brooklyn, New York, 1964)

Actress and choreographer Rosie Pérez is one of the few Hispanic performers who have found a niche in Hollywood. She began her career as a dancer and has choreographed many rap and rhythm-and-blues stage shows and videos. She earned an Emmy nomination for her choreography of the television show *In Living Color*. Pérez has acted in the films *Do the Right Thing* (1989), *White Men Can't Jump* (1992) and *Fearless* (1993), for which she received an Academy Award nomination for best supporting actress.

> Growing up with nine brothers and sisters was an early lesson in assertiveness training. In a family like that, you have to compete for attention.
>
> *Entertainment Weekly* (April 3, 1992)

> I'm very happy with the way things are going for me right now, but I still feel like they're going too slow. I want it all.
>
> *Entertainment Weekly* (April 3, 1992)

> Being a minority you have a responsibility to help other minorities along the way.
>
> *Preview* (April 1992)

> When I dance, it's for me and nobody else. The best moves I come up with are if I'm in a club and nobody's looking at me. I come up with the fly [cool] things.
>
> *GQ* (August 1992)

> I haven't seen anybody who can articulate hip-hop the way I do, in such a lean, crisp way, and still be authentic. There are a lot who try and do it, and it comes off very corny. I still got the flavor.
>
> *GQ* (August 1992)

> The racism, the sexism, I never let it be my problem. It's *their* problem. If I see a door comin' my way, I'm knockin' it down. And if I can't knock down the door, I'm sliding through the window. I'll never let it stop me from what I wanna do.
>
> *Entertainment Weekly* (November 5, 1993)

Tony Pérez (Camagüey, Cuba, 1942)

A first baseman known for his joyful disposition and his uncanny knack for delivering clutch hits, Tony Pérez played in major league baseball for twenty-three years. He is the first Cuban-born player to be voted into the Baseball Hall of Fame.

[On hearing that he had been elected to the Hall of Fame] Are you sure?

New York Times (January 12, 2000)

It's sweet now, when I'm in. It doesn't matter how long I had to wait [to be inducted into the Hall of Fame].

New York Times (January 12, 2000)

[On Caribbeans and baseball] They put their hearts into this. This is about more than baseball.

Kansas City Star (March 24, 2000)

Tony Pérez. Courtesy of the National Baseball Hall of Fame Library, Cooperstown, N.Y.

[On leaving Cuba to play baseball in the United States] It was hard. You miss your country, your mother, your father, your family. I wasn't with my father when he died, or my older sister. It was very difficult.

Cincinnati Enquirer (July 19, 2000)

[On being the first Cuban American elected to the Hall of Fame] It's a great honor. There are a lot of good players who never got a chance. It's a tremendous feeling to be the first one.

Cincinnati Enquirer (July 19, 2000)

Gustavo Pérez Firmat (Havana, Cuba, 1949)

A leading Cuban American scholar and writer, Gustavo Pérez Firmat has published books of prose and poetry, including *Life on the Hyphen: The Cuban-American Way of Life* (1994), *Bilingual Blues* (1995) and *Next Year in Cuba* (1995). He has taught at Duke University and Columbia University.

A few months ago I was translating into Spanish something that I had written in English when I ran into the phrase, "the facts of life." After scrolling my mental Spanish-English dictionary and not coming up with anything that sounded even remotely Castilian, I turned to my reference shelf and, after ruffling around for a while, finally located the phrase in a book of idioms. As it turns out, in Spanish the facts of life are called *los misterios de la vida*. Yes, the same biological drives and imperatives that for the English-speaking world are facts, for us in the Spanish-speaking world are nothing less than mysteries.

anq (American Notes & Queries) (Spring 1997)

Paloma Picasso (Paris, France, 1949)

Raised in France, fashion and jewelry designer Paloma Picasso has homes in Paris and New York. She won the MODA Award for design in 1988.

This [jewelry] is something people can wear, rather than hanging it on the wall or putting it on the table. I like things to be used.

Newsweek (October 20, 1980)

Laffit Pincay Jr. (Panama City, Panama, 1946)

The jockey with the most wins in the history of horseracing, Laffit Pincay Jr.'s thirty-five-year career in racing includes a Kentucky Derby victory, three Belmont Stakes wins, a record five Eclipse Awards as the nation's top jockey and election to racing's Hall of Fame. On December 10, 1999, he broke Bill Shoemaker's record of 8,833 wins.

[After tying Shoemaker's number of wins] I just tied the record of the greatest rider who ever lived.

Lexington Herald-Leader (December 10, 1999)

[The day after breaking Shoemaker's record] I felt great, like I just won the Kentucky Derby.

Lexington Herald-Leader (December 11, 1999)

Miguel Piñero (Gurabo, Puerto Rico, 1946)

An ex-convict who began his writing career in prison, Miguel Piñero is a Nuyorican writer whose plays explore the life of the underclass. He is the author of the play *Short Eyes*, winner of an Obie and the New York Drama Critics Circle Award for best American play in the 1973–74 season.

When you're in prison, you're nowhere being nobody.

Revista Chicano-Riqueña, Vol. 2, No. 1 (1974)

Lou Piniella (Tampa, Florida, 1943)

A player in the major leagues for twenty years, Lou Piniella managed the Cincinnati Reds to the World Series championship in 1990.

If I had had the attitude that I had to play every day to be happy, I wouldn't be here right now. . . . I'd rather be a swing man on a championship team than a regular on another team.

New York Times (May 11, 1978)

I've had a lot of wonderful players and a lot of good memories—great memories, actually.

New York Times (October 18, 2000)

Tito Puente (New York, New York, 1923–2000)

Raised in Harlem, Tito Puente had his breakthrough with the song "Abaniquito" in 1949 and led Latin jazz bands as a percussionist for more than fifty years. An accomplished arranger and composer, "The King" has been a model for several generations of Latin pop artists. Puente won five Grammy Awards and received the National Medal for the Arts in 1997.

People always come up to me and say, "Play that Santana song, 'Oye como va.' " I tell them, "Man, that's a Tito Puente song"—one of four hundred.

Live in concert at The Blue Note, New York City (March 1998)

The word salsa combines all kinds of music into one, like the mambo, the cha-cha, the merengue, all music with Caribbean origins. When they call it salsa, you don't actually define what rhythm is. That's why I don't particularly care for the word. However, sometimes they call me the "King of Salsa," so I'll go along with it, I won't dispute it, as long as they don't call me the "Queen of Salsa."

Jazz from Lincoln Center Web site (1998–99)

Q

Anthony Quinn (Chihuahua, Mexico, 1915–2001)

Born Antonio Quiñones, this Mexican Irish actor appeared in more than 200 films in the United States and Europe. He portrayed a vast range of ethnic types and had one of the most recognized faces and voices in the world. Quinn won two Oscars for best supporting actor.

> I act because I envision a better world than exists. I've seen nothing but wars and strife and hatred, and I'd like to do something about that. I'd like to bring that to people's minds and maybe stimulate them to create a better world. And selfishly, I act because I, too, want to be somebody.
>
> Joan Doviak, *Fourteen Beautiful People* (1970)

> "What does he want?" asked the doctor [Quinn's psychiatrist referring to the actor's alter ego]. What does he want? I thought. "He wants the world," I said. "He wants eternity. He demands things I can't give him. He wants purity and truth." "Can't you give him purity and truth, Tony?" "I give him the truth that's around today. It's the only kind available on the market. But he wants a different brand, one they no longer make."
>
> Anthony Quinn, *The Original Sin* (1972)

> I am very hurt that I am not considered an American actor, extremely hurt by it. But I'm afraid the die has been cast, and I will have to play these ethnic roles—but I must say, I'm very happy, because I get to play Hungarians, I get to play Turkish, I get to play Chinese, I get to play Russians—I get to play a much wider scope of humanity than just, quote, American.
>
> Luis Reyes and Peter Rubie, *Hispanics in Hollywood* (1994)

Ernesto Quiñónez (Ecuador, 1965)

Brought to the United States at the age of eighteen, Ernesto Quiñónez lived in Spanish Harlem. Before writing, he earned his living as a painter of R.I.P. murals for his neighborhood's dearly departed, and as an elementary school teacher. Quiñónez is author of the novel *Bodega Dreams* (2000).

> [On painting R.I.P. murals in Spanish Harlem] Hey, it was a ghetto tradition thing, paying homage to the dead by painting their face on the wall.
>
> *New York Times* (March 15, 2000)

> I know how to cook, sew and iron . . . because here's what my mother told me: "Women leave."
>
> *New York Times* (March 15, 2000)

> I go into West Side Market and little old white ladies tap me on the shoulder and ask where the olive oil is. I'm a professional, a teacher, a writer, but to their eyes I'm still the busboy.
>
> *New York Times* (March 15, 2000)

> [On the supposed flourishing of Latino writers] Go to any Barnes & Noble . . . and there's more John Grisham books than all the Hispanic writers put together. So show me the renaissance.
>
> *New York Times* (March 15, 2000)

José Quintero (Panama City, Panama, 1924–1999)

A stage director who almost singlehandedly revived interest in the playwright Eugene O'Neill, José Quintero staged works by O'Neill and other American dramatists, while nurturing the careers of actors such as Geraldine Page and Jason Robards. He won a Tony as best director, the O'Neill Gold Medal and many other awards. He is a member of the Theatre Hall of Fame.

> The theater . . . can kiss you and applaud you and at the same time break your heart. But there is nothing you can do about it. Nothing you want to do about it. You are in love. What else is there?
>
> José Quintero, *If You Don't Dance They Beat You* (1974)

> [Playwright] Tennessee Williams, whom I had never met, and of whom I was terribly in awe, for I considered him and still do, the greatest living American playwright, came down to see the performance. At the end he stood up and cried, "Bravo, bravo," hitting his silver handled cane on what he thought was the floor, but unfortunately was my foot.
>
> José Quintero, *If You Don't Dance They Beat You* (1974)

If there is anything such as the traffic of souls in the hereafter, mine will go running after his [playwright Eugene O'Neill's], as in life I unknowingly did.

José Quintero, If You Don't Dance They Beat You (1974)

Sofía Quintero (Unknown place and date of birth)

Sofía Quintero is a writer, comedienne and social activist based in New York City. She is the editor of PoliticallyLatino.com and well known for her defense of Puerto Rican rights and multicultural education.

As much love as my people are getting nowadays . . . a Latina like me couldn't cross over. Let's be honest . . . I'm too black, too opinionated, and when I find myself in front of a camera, I have the irresistible urge to keep my clothes *on*.

Ms. (April/May 2000)

No, this latest Latin explosion will have to proceed without me, because I couldn't cross over if I tried. *Diablo* [Devil] if I did, it isn't *me*.

Ms. (April/May 2000)

Finally, Latinos have crossed over, huh? So that's why the most visible Hispanic on prime-time television is a nameless Chihuahua selling anglicized tacos.

Ms. (April/May 2000)

R

Charles B. Rangel (New York, New York, 1930)

An influential congressman from New York State, Charles Rangel has served on many important committees and been an outspoken defender of his constituents. He earned the Purple Heart and Bronze Star in the Korean War.

> We all have a large stake in preserving our democracy, but I maintain that those without power in our society, the black, the brown, the poor of all colors, have the largest stake—not because we have the most to lose, but because we have worked the hardest, and given the most, for what we have achieved.
>
> *Congressional Record* (July 1974)

> Real freedom won't come just from building more jails and putting more cops on the streets; it comes from hope.
>
> *Rangel Reports* (July 1994)

> When things are not going right, you find someone to blame it on.
>
> *Emerge* (1994)

Gina Ravera (San Francisco, California, 1968)

An actress who has played roles on television and in film, Gina Ravera is an African American of Puerto Rican descent.

> There's no separation between health of the mind, body, and spirit. I'm here to celebrate that.
>
> *Latina* (November 1998)

Tey Diana Rebolledo (Las Vegas, New Mexico, 1937)

Professor, editor and critic, Tey Diana Rebolledo teaches at the University of New Mexico. She is editor of several collections by Chicana writers. Rebolledo has been designated an eminent scholar by the New Mexico Commission on Higher Education. She is a fellow of the Aspen Institute and recipient of a research grant from the National Endowment for the Humanities.

> Chicanas who appeared in films, and in literature, had either been whores or saints. They were either the sainted Mother or the hot chili queen. You know, it is simply not true! No women are like that! . . . We're not good or bad, we're a little of everything.
>
> *NuCity* (June 26, 1994)

Bill Richardson (Pasadena, California, 1947)

Born to a Mexican mother and American father, Bill Richardson grew up primarily in Mexico City. He was elected as a United States congressman from New Mexico and governor of the state. Richardson has traveled the world as a diplomat and served as U.S. ambassador to the United Nations and as secretary of energy for former President Bill Clinton.

> That was a major disappointment in my life, not playing major-league baseball. But one year later my elbow went out, and I was washed up as a pitcher. So I guess I made the right choice.
>
> *People* (August 7, 1995)

> For all the criticism I might get, I have done more than most. That's not because of ambition, that's because I want to do things.
>
> Judith Graham (ed.), *Current Biography Yearbook* (1996)

Chita Rivera (Dolores Conchita Figuero del Rivero) (Washington, D.C., 1933)

Dancer and singer Chita Rivera has won two Tony Awards, one for best actress in a musical *(The Rink)* and another for best actress *(Kiss of the Spider Woman)*. Her alma mater, the School of American Ballet, has given her a Lifetime Achievement Award. In 1985 Rivera was inducted into the Television Academy Hall of Fame.

> Dancing is one way of merging with something greater than the dancer.
>
> Matt S. Meier, *Notable Latino Americans* (1997)

Geraldo Rivera (New York, New York, 1943)

Both admired and attacked, talk-show host and journalist Geraldo Rivera may be the most controversial Hispanic in show business. He has been host and correspondent for shows such as *Good Morning America, Good Night America, 20/20* and his own *Geraldo Show* and *Rivera Live*. He has won the George Foster Peabody Award for distinguished achievement in broadcast journalism, two Columbia-Dupont Awards, two Robert F. Kennedy Awards, ten Emmys and three honorary doctorates.

> [When asked what kind of animal he would like to be] A junkyard dog— a greasy, banged-up old German shepherd with a limp, but nobody will mess with.
>
> Matt S. Meier, *Notable Latino Americans* (1997)

José Rivera (Unknown place and date of birth)

This Obie Award-winning playwright is the author of *Marisol* (1992) and other dramas. José Rivera's work has been supported by the National Endowment for the Arts, the Rockefeller Foundation, the Kennedy Center for New American Plays and the Fulbright Commission.

> The city is full of freaks. The criminal lonely. When they leave an apartment, they leave their shadows behind, more alive and active than the cockroaches.
>
> José Rivera, *Lovers of Long Red Hair* (2000)

Tomás Rivera (Crystal City, Texas, 1935–1984)

In addition to writing prose and poetry, Tomás Rivera was an educator who served as chancellor of the University of California, Riverside, from 1980 until his death. His most important work, the novel *. . . y no se lo tragó la tierra/ . . . And the Earth Did Not Part*, won the Premio Quinto Sol in 1970.

> I see my role more as a documentor of that period of time [1945–55] when the migrant worker was living without any kind of protection. There was no legal protection, and without legal protection, there is nothing.
>
> Juan Bruce-Novoa, *Chicano Authors: Inquiry by Interview* (1980)

> To me, they [the migrant workers] were people who searched, and that's an important metaphor in the Americas. . . . I hope I can also be a searcher.
>
> Juan Bruce-Novoa, *Chicano Authors: Inquiry by Interview* (1980)

Arnaldo Roche-Rabell (Santurce, Puerto Rico, 1955)

Painter Arnaldo Roche-Rabell recreates the world of dreams in his neo-expressionist works. He has exhibited his paintings in many countries, especially in the United States and Latin America.

The thing I most cherish is that God gave me the opportunity not only to find myself, but to find myself through my art.

Matt S. Meier, *Notable Latino Americans* (1997)

Alex Rodríguez (New York, New York, 1975)

At the age of twenty-five, baseball player Alex Rodríguez signed a contract with the Texas Rangers for $252 million, making him the highest paid athlete in history. He is known as one of the best all-around players in major-league baseball—a smooth-fielding shortstop, a powerful hitter and a fast base-runner. He is only the third player ever to hit forty home runs and steal forty bases in the same season.

[After signing a contract for $252 million] To me, this is like fake money. You don't know what to do with it.

New York Times (December 13, 2000)

These things change very often. I don't know how long I'll be the highest paid. I don't want to make any presumptions on that.

New York Times (December 13, 2000)

The money's great. . . . I accept the responsibility that goes with it.

New York Times (December 13, 2000)

This has been blown up, all these numbers. Now let's play ball.

Esquire (April 2001)

My talent, what the man upstairs blessed me with . . . the result was my contract. But my work and my love for the game came way before that. People are going to have to make up their own minds. I only worry about the people I love and the people who love me.

Esquire (April 2001)

A lot of Latino kids have nothing. They love it. But to me it was insulting [to have nothing].

Esquire (April 2001)

I have a love affair with the game of baseball that is so sincere and genuine—I don't know. I don't know where it comes from, to be honest with you.

Esquire (April 2001)

Arturo Rodríguez (San Antonio, Texas, 1949)

President of the United Farm Workers of America, Arturo Rodríguez succeeded his father-in-law, César Chávez, in this position.

I alone would never think of replacing César Chávez. He's just an extraordinary human being. . . . But . . . the rest of the leadership is very dedicated, very committed to wanting to see César's dreams come true.
New York Times (July 19, 1993)

Farm workers are so far behind other workers in terms of wages, health plans, the dignity and respect they don't get. That's what drives us.
Current Biography (March 2001)

Cecilia Rodríguez (El Paso, Texas, 1952)

After studying at the University of Texas, Cecilia Rodríguez became a social activist and representative of the Zapatista (indigenous) movement in Mexico. On October 26, 1995, she was raped by three masked men near the Guatemalan border with Mexico, probably in an attempt to silence her support of the Zapatista revolution.

At this point in time, when there's a climate of fear and people are told these problems are from too many dark people, too many gay people and that women should stay home to care for the house, that is in our tradition to say "no." Our tradition is not based on fear.
Current Biography (May 1999)

I have a question . . . [for] those men who raped me. Why did you not kill me? It was a mistake to spare my life. I will not "shut up," I will not stop my work or travel to Chiapas or my work in the United States as a representative of the Zapatistas.
Current Biography (May 1999)

We will never win as long as we allow ourselves to doubt that justice exists only when people are willing to defend it. . . . *May the lesson nourish the wisdom of resistance deep within our hearts.*
Current Biography (May 1999)

Chi Chi Rodríguez (Río Piedras, Puerto Rico, 1935)

One of the great rags to riches stories in the history of golf, Chi Chi (Juan) Rodríguez learned the sport while caddying for tourists in his native Puerto Rico. He has won many important tournaments, including the Denver, Texas and Western Opens and the Dorado Pro-Am. His dedicated fans are known as Chi Chi's Bandidos. He is founder of the Chi Chi Rodríguez Youth Foundation in Clearwater, Florida.

Golf is the most fun you can have without taking your clothes off.
Robert Byrne, *1911 Best Things Anybody Ever Said* (1988)

Eloy Rodríguez (Edinburg, Texas, 1947)

Born into an extended family in Hidalgo County, south Texas, Eloy Rodríguez has sixty-seven cousins, of whom sixty-four obtained college degrees. He is an environmental biologist, one of the world's leading plant chemists and also one of the creators of a new field, zoopharmacognosy, or the study of self-medication by animals. His larger research interest is *yerbas* (medicinal herbs). Rodríguez is also one of the founders of Kids Investigating and Discovering Science (KIDS), a program for underprivileged students at the University of California, Irvine.

[My primary school teachers] hit me on my hands and made me write on the blackboard, "I will not speak Spanish." They had this idea that your brain didn't have the capacity to handle two languages.

New York Times Magazine (December 18, 1994)

You know, I used to pick cotton as a kid. Cotton, strawberries, cherries. And I hated it—I *hated* it! I swore I'd never do it again. It's why you got an education. And look at me now. I've got a Ph.D. and I'm still collecting plants for a living.

New York Times Magazine (December 18, 1994)

We were so poor that crime really didn't pay. It really didn't. I mean, who do you steal from in a neighborhood like ours?

New York Times Magazine (December 18, 1994)

I always say I saw my first snowflake before I saw my first Hispanic scientist.

New York Times Magazine (December 18, 1994)

The research bug got to me, the passion, the excitement of science. Once it gets you, you can't let go of it.

American Biology Teacher (May 1996)

Yerbas do work. . . . It's like being at the opening of the cosmos.

Latino Web site (1997)

A great scientist, man or woman, is one who has great compassion for humanity and Life, and never forgets his roots and ancestors.

Original quotation for this book (January 31, 2000)

I call myself a Chicano.

Original quotation for this book (January 31, 2000)

Never let yourself be discouraged by negative and mean-spirited people.

Current Biography (May 2000)

Eloy Rodríguez. Photo by Frank DiMeo. Courtesy of Cornell University.

Education will get you what you want in life, but you must work at it.
Current Biography (May 2000)

I didn't pull myself up by the bootstraps, I had a lot of help from my family.

Latino Web site (2000)

Put a Barbie [doll] next to just about anything and meaning will rear its ugly head. This little pink lady is just too well known, and way too voluptuous to be perceived as just an object. She leaps into our psyches and roams freely in our subconscious, along with mom, the mother superior and the Virgin Mary (yes, I was raised as a Catholic).

My Personal Page Web site (2000)

Paul Rodríguez (Culiacán, Mexico)

As the main character of *A.K.A. Pablo*, Paul Rodríguez was the first Mexican American to have a starring role in a network television show in the United States. He is a successful comedian who has also appeared in movies such as *Born in East L.A.* (1987) and *Made in America* (1993). Rodríguez owns the company that produced the movie *A Million to Juan* (1994).

> If I die today, I'm proud of one thing. I was in Washington D.C. with my son and in the corner [of the Smithsonian Museum] there is the first starring role of a Mexican-American in a network show, and it's "A.K.A. Pablo." And you press a button and a skinny guy that looks like me comes out.
>
> *Latin Style* (September 1999)

> I love the freedom [of stand-up comedy]. I love the art of it and the power of it; to use humor and make people think.
>
> *Latin Style* (September 1999)

> In the future you're going to tell me you want a galaxy without salsa? What kind of future is that?
>
> *Latin Style* (September 1999)

> I know in my heart that we're in a golden age of Latino comedians.
>
> *Latin Style* (September 1999)

> Let's face it, even when Latino actors aren't hot in the movies or when we're not on American television, our music has always been there.
>
> *Latin Style* (September 1999)

> A lot of people criticize me for my poor Spanish. . . . But rather than feeling hurt, getting angry or giving up, I decided to find a tutor, because I do not want to lose a part of my roots.
>
> *Cristina* (October 2000)

> By comparison, for what I was able to make my little film for, and what it has grossed financially, "A Million to Juan" has become my Latino "Jurassic Park."
>
> *Qué Pasa* Web site (2000)

> It is my belief that Latinos in show business have to be self-sufficient and creative while aggressively attempting to penetrate post-mogul Hollywood. Self-starting is becoming the path to serious studio support, and I hope that through my little company, we can continue to create successful projects that will stand on their own, and ultimately open the door to that next project.
>
> *Qué Pasa* Web site (2000)

Richard Rodríguez (San Francisco, California, 1944)

The author of *Hunger of Memory* (1981), *Brown* (2002) and many other books, Richard Rodríguez works as an editor at the Pacific News Service in San Francisco, is a contributing editor to *Harper's* and the *Los Angeles Times* and is a regular commentator on *The News Hour with Jim Lehrer* on PBS.

> I was *un católico* before I was a Catholic. That is, I acquired my earliest sense of the Church . . . through my parents' Mexican Catholicism. It was in Spanish that I first learned to pray.
>
> *Hunger of Memory. The Education of Richard Rodríguez: An Autobiography* (1981)

> I refuse to accept my generation's romanticism about discovering "roots." The trouble with that is it somehow holds children accountable for maintaining their culture, and freezes them into thinking of themselves as Mexicans or as Chinese or as blacks. But culture is an extraordinary progression of ancestral memories and individual experience.
>
> *People* (August 16, 1982)

> People have accused me of losing my heritage. That assumes heritage is this little suitcase I carry with me, with tortillas and a little Mexican cowboy suit inside, and that one day I lost it at a Greyhound bus depot. The fact is, culture survives whether you want it to or not.
>
> *People* (August 16, 1982)

> The U.S. reached under Mexico's skirt every chance he got.
>
> Ana Castillo (ed.), *Goddess of the Americas. La Diosa de las Américas. Writings on the Virgin of Guadalupe* (1996)

> By the twenty-first century, the locus of the Catholic Church, by virtue of its numbers, will be Latin America, by which time Catholicism itself will have assumed the aspect of the Virgin of Guadalupe. Brown skin.
>
> Ana Castillo (ed.), *Goddess of the Americas. La Diosa de las Américas. Writings on the Virgin of Guadalupe* (1996)

Robert Rodríguez (San Antonio, Texas, 1969)

After studying film at the University of Texas, Robert Rodríguez and his wife, Elizabeth Abellán, produced their first feature film, the popular *El Mariachi* (1993), directed by Rodríguez himself. Since then they have done *Roadracers* (1994) and *Desperado, Four Rooms,* and *From Dusk Till Dawn* (all 1995), *The Faculty* (1998), *Spy Kids* (2001) and *Spy Kids II* (2002). Rodríguez and Abellán are founders and owners of Los Hooligans Productions.

Some critic told me I'd better be careful, because you just get one shot. I told him I can always go back to making Mexican action movies. I keep a separate savings account with $7,000 in it, just in case.

New York Times (February 21, 1993)

We had a school bus, a pit bull, a motorcycle, two bars, and a ranch. So I wrote a script around those elements [for *El Mariachi*].

Vanity Fair (March 1993)

One guy in New York made me sound like a genius. He said I obviously took this *[El Mariachi]* from a literary classic, and I was, like, "I don't even read, you know!"

Washington Post (April 3, 1993)

I accepted the fact that I would never be a rocket scientist. I knew that if I couɪd just draw cartoons or make little movies on the side, I would be happy the rest of my life.

Washington Post (April 3, 1993)

Lina Romay (Brooklyn, New York, 1921)

The daughter of a Mexican diplomat, Elena "Lina" Romay became the lead singer for Xavier Cugat's famous band before being signed by MGM. She was featured in musicals with Cugat and also played dramatic roles.

I don't want to be typed as a Latin or anything else.

Hollywood Studio (April 1985)

When the movies get a Latin girl they always try to make a spitfire out of her, another Lupe Velez [early Mexican American film star]. That's not any more typical of a Latin girl than Betty Hutton is of an American girl.

Hollywood Studio (April 1985)

César Romero (New York, New York, 1907)

The son of Cuban immigrants, actor César Romero played the Latin lover in Hollywood films from the 1930s through the 1960s. He was a grandson of the great leader of Cuba's struggle for independence, José Martí. Romero is remembered as the actor who established the film personality of the Cisco Kid.

[On Evita and Juan Perón, then first lady and president of Argentina] I was sitting next to Evita during the luncheon, and she said to me, "Why do the people in your country call my husband a dictator? He is not a dictator, he is a patriot." She turned to her husband and said, "Is not that right, Juan? You're not a dictator," and he said, "Yes, my dear."

Luis Reyes and Peter Rubie, *Hispanics in Hollywood* (1994)

Linda Ronstadt (Tuscon, Arizona, 1946)

Of German and Mexican ancestry, singer Linda Ronstadt has mastered many styles of music, ranging from pop standards to rock, jazz, blues, big band classics and Mexican folk songs. She was the top female vocalist of the 1980s, has received many Grammy Awards and has appeared on the cover of magazines such as *Time, Rolling Stone, People* and *Us.*

> It was really hot in Tucson in the summer, and we had a cement floor, and I used to lie on the floor because it was cool, with my cheek to the radio. I had grooves on my cheeks. I was about five when I started doing that.
>
> *Time* (February 1977)

> I'd take three giant steps toward an early death if I could find one good song.
>
> *Time* (February 1977)

> I love sex as much as I love music, and I think it's as hard to do.
>
> Mark Bego, *Linda Ronstadt* (1990)

> People tend to lump Hispanic cultures together. They think Ricky Ricardo would have been happy dancing the tango to a mariachi band.
>
> *TV Guide* (December 21, 1991)

> When we were little, we spoke Spanish at home, but the schools pounded it out of us pretty early. There was an antibilingual attitude. So my Spanish is very rudimentary—child's Spanish, really.
>
> *Parade* (December 22, 1991)

> It's very important for me not to have my middle age be a repeat of my youth, and my old age to not be a repeat of my middle age.
>
> *Weekend Australian* (July 1998)

> I know there are certain things that I must do so that I won't be kept awake late at night when I am in my 60's and 70's saying, "I wish I'd done that."
>
> *Weekend Australian* (July 1998)

> I've decided that I'll do whatever I want to do and I've always tried not to have commercial considerations.
>
> *Weekend Australian* (July 1998)

> I hear music. It's what I do. If I'd been good at building skyscrapers, I would have done that.
>
> *Mr. Showbiz Interview* Web site (2000)

Margarita Roque (El Paso, Texas, 1946)

After working with the Women's Vote Project and the Churches' Committee for Voter Registration, Margarita Roque became executive director of the Congressional Hispanic Caucus, a bipartisan organization.

> I was always the trouble maker. If you don't speak out about your problems, you're not going to get results.
> Diane Telgen and Jim Kamp (eds.), *Notable Hispanic American Women* (1993)

Ileana Ros-Lehtinen (Havana, Cuba, 1952)

The first Latina elected to the Florida state House of Representatives, the youngest person and the first Hispanic to serve in the state Senate and the first Latina and Cuban American elected to the U.S. House of Representatives (Republican), Ileana Ros-Lehtinen has served as a member of

Congresswoman Ileana Ros-Lehtinen. Courtesy of the U.S. House of Representatives.

the critical House Foreign Affairs Committee. After graduating with a master's degree from Florida International University, she founded a private elementary school that she both owned and operated. "Ileanita," as she is known to her many supporters, is one of the most important Hispanic politicians in the United States.

> Now more than ever, we Hispanic women must re-energize and refocus our efforts to realize the vast potential that lies within our grasp.
>
> *Vista* (February 4, 1992)

> [The Hispanic woman] is an accomplished writer, or a computer programmer, or an attorney, or a doctor, as well as a loving wife and mother.
>
> *Hispanic* (August 1992)

> While our diverse traditions give us the different rhythms of the salsa, tango, and merengue, and interesting foods like tortillas and black beans and rice, we share a common interest in our culture, our native language, and our traditions.
>
> Foreword, Amy L. Unterburger (ed.), *Who's Who among Hispanic Americans* (1992)

> It is no secret that the success of the Hispanic individual begins with the Hispanic family. Most often, grandparents and aunts and uncles add to the immediate family, creating quite a gathering at the most minor of events. Within these families, parents have fostered warmth and unity combined with responsibility and integrity, building the foundation on which we continue to make a difference in the lives of others.
>
> Foreword, Amy L. Unterburger (ed.), *Who's Who among Hispanic Americans* (1992)

> We need to encourage more Latinas to become active in public administration and to run for office. There's a "machismo" myth that says Hispanic men won't vote for female candidates. But that's untrue. In recent elections, Latinos of both sexes have elected women to Congress and to state legislatures.
>
> *George* (July 1999)

Edward R. Roybal (Albuquerque, New Mexico, 1916–1993)

First elected to the U.S. Congress for California's twenty-fifth district in 1962, Edward R. Roybal chaired many committees in the House, including the powerful Appropriations Committee. He was also chairman of the Congressional Hispanic Caucus and introduced legislation for the first bilingual education act on the federal level.

Edward R. Roybal. Courtesy of the Center for Southwest Research, General Library, University of New Mexico.

I want to be remembered as an advocate of good health, good education, and good nursing.

Matt S. Meier, *Notable Latino Americans* (1997)

Lucille Roybal-Allard (Los Angeles, California, 1941)

Representative of California's thirty-third congressional district, Lucille Roybal-Allard is a political pioneer in many ways. Daughter of California congressman Edward R. Roybal, in 1992 she became the first Mexican American woman to be elected to the U.S. House of Representatives. She was also the first Latina in history on the powerful House Appropriations Committee. Finally, Roybal-Allard was the first woman to chair the Congressional Hispanic Caucus. She received Las Primeras Award from the Mexican American Women's National Association.

Congresswoman Lucille Roybal-Allard. Courtesy of the U.S. House of Representatives.

When my sister and I would go to a dance where people might not know who we were, we used to decide on a different last name so we could just be anonymous and have fun.

Civic Center News Source (January 13, 1992)

I remember as a freshman in college in a political science class I raised my hand to answer a question and after I finished the professor said "Well, now we know what your father thinks," and went on to the next student.

Civic Center News Source (January 13, 1992)

People may be your enemies today on one issue, but they may be your allies tomorrow on another issue. So I've learned to work well with groups on both sides of the aisle, even with those who I oppose bitterly on particular issues.

Hispanic (March 1992)

Vicki Ruiz (Atlanta, Georgia, 1955)

Vicki Ruiz has had a meteoric career in the American Academy, writing several important works on the history of Mexican women in the United States. She is Andrew W. Mellon Professor of the Humanities at the Claremont Graduate School.

> My mother was a survivor, and she found great joy in working and helping out. She was also a wonderful storyteller.
>
> Diane Telgen and Jim Kamp (eds.), *Notable Hispanic American Women* (1993)

S

Luis Omar Salinas (Robstown, Texas, 1937)

Raised in Texas and Mexico, poet Luis Omar Salinas remembers writing his earliest verses in a sanatorium.

> A man can go mad with too many dreams and be mad for not having any at all.
>
> Wolfgang Binder (ed.), *Partial Autobiographies: Interviews with Twenty Chicano Poets* (1985)

Raúl Salinas (San Antonio, Texas, 1934)

After spending time in juvenile centers, poet Raúl Salinas was incarcerated in Soledad prison, where he belonged to a writers' group. He has worked for El Centro de la Raza in Seattle.

> I find a strong need to see myself as a Chicano-*Indio*. *Indio* is where my roots are and what will eventually save me from the Hispanization of our people, which in the terms of the U.S. government is another form of genocide to some of us.
>
> Wolfgang Binder (ed.), *Partial Autobiographies: Interviews with Twenty Chicano Poets* (1985)

Edwin Sánchez (Arecibo, Puerto Rico, 1955)

A well-known playwright, Edwin Sánchez has won the William Morris Agency Fellowship, the Eugene O'Neill Scholarship, the Princess Grace Playwriting Award and the ASCAP Cole Porter Award.

> The most important thing about the character [in a play] is finding out what song speaks to me about them. Like if [the characters] were walk-

ing down the street and they heard a song, they would stop and say, "That's my song! That's my song!" And I go, "Okay, now I know the character."

Urban Latino, No. 22 (1999)

[When asked to give advice to aspiring playwrights] Oh, it's simple. Write. Write. Write.

Urban Latino, No. 22 (1999)

Elisa Maria Sánchez (Central, New Mexico)

Born and raised in the small mining town of Central (known later as Santa Clara), Elisa Maria Sánchez went on to study at Western New Mexico University and Baruch College of the City University of New York. She is an activist and president of MANA, a national Latina organization.

We are caught in the rhetoric and roots of our past rather than using the strengths of our Spanish and Indian roots to move toward change and the future.

Joseph M. Palmisano (ed.), *Notable Hispanic American Women*, Book II (1998)

Sonia Sánchez (Birmingham, Alabama, 1934)

Poet, mother, activist and teacher, Sonia Sánchez lectures on African American culture, racial justice, women's liberation and peace.

I write to keep in contact with our ancestors and to spread truth to people.

Claudia Tate, *Black Women Writers at Work* (1985)

In order to be a true revolutionary, you must understand love. Love, sacrifice, and death.

Claudia Tate, *Black Women Writers at Work* (1985)

So much of growing up is an unbearable waiting. A constant longing for another time. Another season.

Sonia Sánchez, *Under a Soprano Sky* (1987)

The words loved me and I loved them in return.

Sonia Sánchez, *Under a Soprano Sky* (1987)

Arturo Sandoval (Havana, Cuba, 1949)

Arturo Sandoval is a jazz trumpeter.

There is a lot in the news that makes you feel anger and hate; but Latin music shows people the sunny side of the street. Our culture is about giving people the desire to enjoy life and be optimistic. We put the spice in the soup.

George (July 1999)

Denise Sandoval (Unknown place and date of birth)

A scholar who wrote the first dissertation on lowriders (the road-hugging cars first customized by Chicanos), Denise Sandoval has also been curator of an exhibit on her favorite vehicles.

Lowriders are part of the historical memory of this city [Los Angeles]. . . . It was really an important form of expression for Chicanos. I see more pride among the guys who do this than I do even among students I teach.

New York Times (February 19, 2000)

Carlos Santana (Autlán, Jalisco, Mexico, 1947)

The Woodstock festival in 1969 sent guitarist, bandleader and composer Carlos Santana to the top of the music charts and into the mainstream of rock and roll. In 2000 he tied Michael Jackson's record for the most Grammys in a single year (eight). With his wife, Deborah Santana, he is the founder of the Milagro Foundation, which provides financial assistance for educational, medical and housing needs of children all over the world.

Carlos Santana. Photo by Paul Freehauf. Courtesy of Photofest.

[When asked by record producer Clive Davis what he wanted to do in his new album] Mr. Davis, I want to reconnect the molecules with the light.

Time (October 25, 1999)

[After a vision of the Virgin of Guadalupe] My heart was transformed into a bird of fire that only wanted to fly and go toward her. . . . I started to cry—I'd never cried before—and she said: "Calm down, breathe, I am very proud and happy with you."

Lexington Herald-Leader (December 10, 1999)

Live up to your convictions.

Carlos Santana Web site (1999)

You walk in grace or you walk in fear. You can't have it both ways.

Carlos Santana Web site (1999)

If you follow your dreams, your inspirations, and your aspirations you'll get where you wanna be.

WHAS Radio, Louisville, Kentucky (February 23, 2000)

Music is the vehicle for the magic of healing.

San Francisco Chronicle (February 24, 2000)

You can cuss or you can pray with the guitar.

Rolling Stone (March 16, 2000)

Geniuses don't have time to think how it's going to be received. Real bona fide geniuses of this century—Miles Davis, Picasso—they don't have time to think whether people like it or not, is it morally right, will God like it?

Rolling Stone (March 16, 2000)

If you carry joy in your heart, you can heal any moment. There is no person that love cannot heal; there is no soul that love cannot save.

Rolling Stone (March 16, 2000)

My reality is that God speaks to you every day. There's an inner voice, and when you hear it, you get a little tingle in your medulla oblongata at the back of your neck, a little shiver.

Rolling Stone (March 16, 2000)

My reality is my reality. I'm not going to deny it. I'm not going to deny it all. I stand in front of people. Behold my reality.

Rolling Stone (March 16, 2000)

Don't think so much before you play. Just let it flow. . . . That's the best kind of music, when you go beyond gravity and time and thinking. Not many mortals do it. I am just trying to get there. Every night I'm just trying to get there, man.

Rolling Stone (March 16, 2000)

From my inner dreams and meditations I received instructions from an entity—an angel—I call Metatron. He said, "I will help you if you will help me solder back molecules with the light."

Grammy (Spring/Summer 2000)

We believe in a brighter future for the children of this planet. We also know that we must accelerate equality, justice, compassion, beauty, grace and excellence, kindness and gentleness in the here and now.

UCLA Magazine (Summer 2001)

George Santayana (Madrid, Spain, 1863–1952)

Although he was born and died in Europe, George Santayana spent half his life in the United States, where he studied and taught philosophy at Harvard University. He was a poet and novelist as well as a philosopher and critic. Santayana can be considered the first Hispanic to have a successful career in American academia.

Those who cannot remember the past are condemned to repeat it.

George Santayana, *The Life of Reason* (1905–6)

A musical education is necessary for musical judgment. What most people relish is hardly music: it is rather a drowsy revery relieved by nervous thrills.

George Santayana, *The Life of Reason* (1905–6)

Truth is a jewel which should not be painted over; but it may be set to advantage and shown in a good light.

George Santayana, *The Life of Reason* (1905–6)

An ideal cannot wait for its realization to prove its validity.

George Santayana, *The Life of Reason* (1905–6)

In imagination, not in perception, lies the substance of experience, while knowledge and reason are but its chastened and ultimate form.

George Santayana, *The Life of Reason* (1905–6)

Perhaps the only true dignity of man is his capacity to despise himself.

George Santayana, *Spinoza's Ethics* (1910)

The American talks about money because that is the symbol and measure he has at hand for success, intelligence, and power; but, as to money itself, he makes, loses, spends, and gives it away with a very light heart.

George Santayana, *Character and Opinion in the United States* (1920)

Society is like the air, necessary to breathe, but insufficient to live on.

George Santayana, *Little Essays* (1920)

To turn events into ideas is the function of literature.

George Santayana, *Little Essays* (1920)

There is no cure for birth or death save to enjoy the interval.

George Santayana, *Soliloquies in England* (1922)

Religion in its humility restores man to his only dignity, the courage to live by grace.

George Santayana, *Dialogues in Limbo* (1925)

America is the greatest of opportunities and the worst of influences.

George Santayana, *The Last Puritan* (1935)

An artist may visit a museum but only a pedant can live there.

Lawrence J. Peter, *Peter's Quotations: Ideas for Our Time* (1977)

Our friends are that part of the human race with which one can be human.

Lawrence J. Peter, *Peter's Quotations: Ideas for Our Time* (1977)

[His final words, when asked if he was suffering] Yes, my friend. But my anguish is entirely physical. There are no more difficulties whatsoever.

Daniel Cory, *Santayana: The Later Years* (1963)

Enrico Mario Santí (Santiago, Cuba, 1950)

After studying at Vanderbilt and Yale Universities, Enrico Mario Santí taught at Cornell University, Georgetown University and the University of Kentucky, where he is the William T. Bryan Professor of Hispanic Studies. He is the author of numerous books on Latin American literature and culture. Santí also writes poetry.

My first sabbatical semester, during the winter of 1980, I spent in Tampa, where my parents lived among a large Cuban-American community. My first day back, delighted to be home from a cruel winter, I went shopping for food in one of the local Cuban grocery stores. After picking up my café cubano, my plátanos [plantains], and my black beans, happy as a tropical bird, I went up to choose some meat cuts. The butcher, a Cuban guy I had met right there the previous summer, asked me how come I was there at that time of year. I told him I was *"de sabático"* (on sabbatical). With eyes wide open, he remarked: *"Coño* [Hell], I didn't know you were Jewish."

Original quotation for this book (February 2000)

Esmeralda Santiago (Santurce, Puerto Rico, 1948)

Author of the memoir *When I Was Puerto Rican* (1994) and the novel *América's Dream* (1996), Esmeralda Santiago is a storyteller who speaks for women trapped in a cycle of violence and tedious work. She grew up in Puerto Rico and New York, then studied at Harvard University and Sarah Lawrence College. Santiago and her husband have created a film production company that has made award-winning documentaries.

> I had my last guava the day we left Puerto Rico. It was large and juicy, almost red in the center, and so fragrant that I didn't want to eat it because I would lose the smell.
>
> *When I Was Puerto Rican* (1994)

> Men, I was learning, were *sinvergüenzas*, which meant they had no shame and indulged in behavior that never failed to surprise women but caused them much suffering. Chief among the sins of men was the other woman, who was always a *puta*, a whore. . . . *Putas*, I guessed, lived in luxury in the city on the money that *sinvergüenza* husbands did not bring home to their long-suffering wives and barefoot children. *Putas* wore lots of perfume, jewelry, dresses cut low to show off their breasts, high heels to pump up their calves, and hair spray.
>
> *When I Was Puerto Rican* (1994)

> The things that I thought were really crucial in my life hardly figure in my writing.
>
> *New Letters on the Air*, NPR (March 5, 2000)

> [At a performing arts high school] I discovered that I could do Indian classical dance. It really did change my life because I really had nothing. . . . And all of a sudden I found that I could express myself. I could be graceful and beautiful and I could be strong because it required enormous amounts of stamina and strength. It did give me another vision of who I was. It helped guide me for the rest of my life.
>
> *New Letters on the Air*, NPR (March 5, 2000)

> And people would ask me every day, when I would take my son out in his stroller: "Where are you from?" And I began to think, Wait a second . . . are they asking me because they are interested, or are they asking because I look as if I do not belong in this town?
>
> *New Letters on the Air*, NPR (March 5, 2000)

> The constant question of "Where are you from?" . . . led me to write.
>
> *New Letters on the Air*, NPR (March 5, 2000)

> I couldn't tell you what the difference is between Hispanic and Latino . . . and it doesn't matter to me. And it doesn't matter if people label

me. It isn't something I have any control over. I am who I am and people will just have to find their way of dealing with that.

New Letters on the Air, NPR (March 5, 2000)

I think that [ethnicity] should not be all we worry about. I'd like to see life concerns that have nothing to do with ethnicity.

El Andar (Spring 2000)

What is the sense of blaming myself for what I've just done, if it's not going to change the outcome of what I'm doing right now?

El Andar (Spring 2000)

A lot of what I write is almost documenting my life for other kids, for the next generation.

El Andar (Spring 2000)

Cristina Saralegui (Havana, Cuba, 1948)

El Show de Cristina, hosted by Cristina Saralegui, was the highest-rated talk show on Spanish-language television during the 1990s. A former ed-

Cristina Saralegui. Photo by Nolasco. Courtesy of Cristina Saralegui Enterprises, Inc.

itor for the Hispanic edition of *Cosmopolitan*, this Cuban American performer and producer also has a popular radio program called *Cristina Opina* [Cristina Says] and publishes the monthly magazine *Cristina*.

That's the secret of our marriage. Be together and talk about everything twenty-four hours a day.

Más (July/August 1991)

I want to have fun while I work. Life is not only work and work, you also have to do what most appeals to you.

La Opinión (October 20, 1991)

We do the show to help Hispanics here. Once you cross the border you are an immigrant, not a tourist. This is where our kids grow up and we have to be concerned with community.

Hispanic (November 1991)

Here [in the United States], if an Anglo woman makes more money than her husband, it's a problem. But for a Hispanic woman, it destroys her whole house.

Chicago Tribune (May 31, 1992)

The Cubans are just my tribe. Hispanics are my people. Cuba is my roots, but this [the United States] is my country.

Chicago Tribune (May 31, 1992)

At the beginning they said "it [the show] won't work. You're a Cuban woman. You have a Cuban accent. How dare you represent us [Hispanics] because you're so white? I understand that brown is beautiful, but so is white, pink, or whatever you are."

Chicago Tribune (May 31, 1992)

After the first show the letters started coming in and they told me stuff that I would not tell my pastor, my gynecologist or my husband.

Chicago Tribune (May 31, 1992)

Whenever we are on the "Donahue" show or whatever, we try to be very American, rather than Italian, Jewish, Irish, Hispanic, or black, [but] I want my guests to be what they really are, because diversity makes this country fun and great.

New York Times (July 26, 1992)

Nothing I've done in my life has been normal.

Cristina Saralegui, *¡Cristina! Confessions of a Blond* (1998)

Chance . . . I am convinced . . . is the angel's language for communicating with us.

Cristina Saralegui, *¡Cristina! Confessions of a Blond* (1998)

For us, *salsa* is a music that we dance to and that gladdens our spirit, not something that we pour on our food.

Cristina Saralegui, *¡Cristina! Confessions of a Blond* (1998)

Success has very little to do with luck.

Cristina Saralegui, *¡Cristina! Confessions of a Blond* (1998)

Convince yourself that self-discipline is the key to success.

Cristina Saralegui, *¡Cristina! Confessions of a Blond* (1998)

Action is the cure for depression. When you feel depressed, get up, take a shower or bath, dress and go out for a walk.

Cristina Saralegui, *¡Cristina! Confessions of a Blond* (1998)

Latin women are liberated from the neck up, not from the neck down. Our most important organ is located between the ears, not between the legs.

Cristina Saralegui, *¡Cristina! Confessions of a Blond* (1998)

I believe that the key to the program's *[El Show de Cristina]* success is that I speak the truth and share my problems with the audience. You can't be like a piece of candy and try to please everyone. We all have secrets, and the audience appreciates it when I tell them mine.

Cristina Saralegui, *¡Cristina! Confessions of a Blond* (1998)

People say that you can't have everything in life. That's a lie! You can have everything (or at least a lot), as long as you know how to choose. Life is nothing but an endless rosary of choices and lessons, one after another.

Cristina Saralegui, *¡Cristina! Confessions of a Blond* (1998)

Americans have changed a lot in the last five years. They know salsa is something that Cubans dance and Mexicans eat.

Current Biography (January 1999)

The common denominator all Latinos have is that we want some respect. That's what we're all fighting for.

New York Times (June 23, 1999)

[My goal is] raising my people's self-esteem and knowledge quotient so they can succeed in this very competitive country, and making them feel that they are supported in their efforts.

New York Times (June 23, 1999)

When I married my second husband, I wanted to have a child. . . . The doctor told me "Take out your uterus," and I told him: "You know what? This uterus is mine, not yours." I changed doctors and now I have a 13-year old son.

New York Times (June 23, 1999)

Arthur Alfonso Schomburg (San Juan, Puerto Rico, 1874–1936)

Educated in his native Puerto Rico and at St. Thomas College in the Virgin Islands, Arthur Alfonso Schomburg moved to the United States and became a noted bibliophile, curator, writer and Mason. He cofounded the Negro Society for Social Research in 1911 and became president of the American Negro Academy in 1922. Schomburg's personal collection forms the basis of the New York Public Library's Schomburg Center for Research in Black Culture.

> The American Negro must remake his past in order to make his future.
> "The Negro Digs up His Past" in Alain Locke (ed.), *The New Negro. An Interpretation* (1968)

> The bigotry of civilization which is the taproot of intellectual prejudice begins far back and must be corrected at its source.
> "The Negro Digs up His Past" in Alain Locke (ed.), *The New Negro. An Interpretation* (1968)

> History must restore what slavery took away.
> "The Negro Digs up His Past" in Alain Locke (ed.), *The New Negro. An Interpretation* (1968)

> Pride of race is the antidote to prejudice.
> "The Negro Digs up His Past" in Alain Locke (ed.), *The New Negro. An Interpretation* (1968)

> An ounce of fact is worth a pound of controversy.
> "The Negro Digs up His Past" in Alain Locke (ed.), *The New Negro. An Interpretation* (1968)

Pancho Segura (Guayaquil, Ecuador, 1921)

Tennis fans of the 1940s and 1950s cannot forget the bowlegged player with the two-handed shots, Francisco "Pancho" Segura. He won three intercollegiate titles at the University of Miami. Later he won two World Professional championships.

> An hour of practice is worth five hours of foot-dragging.
> *Infoplease* Web site (2000)

Selena (Selena Quintanilla Pérez) (Lake Jackson, Texas, 1971–1995)

Selena Quintanilla Pérez was the beloved queen of Tejano music until she was shot to death at the age of twenty-three. Her albums continue to sell in both the United States and Latin America.

Never in my dreams would I have thought I would become this big. I am freaking out.

Time (April 10, 1995)

I've always believed in the saying, "Good things come to those who wait." So we've been waiting patiently.

Clint Richmond, *Selena!* (1995)

This is all like a dream and I don't want to be woken up.

TelvisionCity Web site (1999)

Andrés Serrano (New York, New York, 1950)

A controversial artist, Andrés Serrano has exhibited his work in major museums throughout the world.

I had red and white and, quite frankly, I needed a third color to add to my palate. . . . I turned to urine . . . a quite vivid and vibrant color.

New York Times (August 16, 1989)

Shakira (Barranquilla, Colombia, 1977)

Fusing a variety of pop styles, Shakira combines rock, reggae and Latin elements in her music.

We are made of fusion. It's what determines our identity: the way in one mouthful we take rice, *plátanos* [plantains], meat.

Newsweek (July 12, 1999)

Martin Sheen (Ramón Estévez) (Dayton, Ohio, 1940)

Born the seventh of ten children to a Spanish immigrant father and an Irish immigrant mother, actor Martin Sheen first attracted critics' attention on Broadway. He has played leading roles in many films, including *Apocalypse Now,* and in television shows such as *West Wing.* He is also a social activist who has participated in antinuclear campaigns. Rare in Hollywood, Sheen has been married to the same woman for more than thirty years and is father to four children, all of whom are actors.

My name is still Ramón Estévez on my passport, my birth certificate, driver's license, everything, every official document. [Sheen's] just a stage name.

Matt S. Meier, *Notable Latino Americans* (1997)

I don't believe in God, but I do believe that Mary was his mother.

Mr. Showbiz Web site (2000)

Laura Angélica Simón (Mexico, 1965)

Laura Angélica Simón was a school teacher in Los Angeles when she made the film *Fear and Learning at Hoover Elementary*, inspired by her frustration with the 1994 passage of California's Proposition 187. Her work won the Freedom of Expression Award at the Sundance Film Festival and aired nationally on PBS. Simón and actress Meg Ryan helped start the Children's Basic Needs Fund for her inner-city school.

> I just love being Mexican. I love being an immigrant. I love being an American.
>
> Joseph M. Palmisano (ed.), *Notable Hispanic American Women*, Book II (1998)

Jimmy Smits (New York, New York, 1958)

Emmy-winning television and film actor Jimmy Smits played Hispanic lawyer Víctor Sifuentes on the popular television series *L.A. Law* and Bobby Simone on *NYPD Blue*. His most popular film to date is *My Family* (1995).

> I am an American and Latino; I can't separate this dual identity. It's not like asking, "What's it like to be an American in Paris?" Latinos are Americans. We root for the Yankees, the Dodgers, the Astros. We shop the after-Christmas sales. We truck out to the discount malls to buy our kids tennis shoes. We scout. We fish. We salsa.
>
> *George* (July 1999)

> My father was a major disciplinarian. "You will go to school. You will stay in your room three hours to do your homework. You will make yourself better." Hey, that's as American as apple pie.
>
> *San Francisco Examiner* (March 28, 2000)

> You can't tell the kids in acting classes, "If you stay with it you're going to wind up being Tom Cruise." But you can point to your own experience and say, "It can be done."
>
> *San Francisco Examiner* (March 28, 2000)

> As far as the music landscape is concerned, we [Latinos] are now a part of America.
>
> *San Francisco Examiner* (March 28, 2000)

> I remember breaking into my daughter's piggy bank to get money so I could have car fare, for me—so that I could go on an audition for a job. That screwed me up. . . . Things were that bad. But I got the job and replaced the money.
>
> *Latin Style* (April 2000)

Jimmy Smits. Photo by Francois Duhamel. Courtesy of Photofest.

Octavio Solís (El Paso, Texas, 1958)

Writer, actor, director and teacher Octavio Solís has worked for Teatro
Dallas and the Dallas Theatre Center. In 1988 he was named Reader's Poll
Best Playwright by the *Dallas Observer;* in 1990 he won the Hispanic Play-
wrights Project Award.

> I needed some discipline in my life. Army's a good place to start. The
> chain of command is clear, PFC [private first-class] to God.
>
> *El Otro* [The Other] (1997)

> There are things our bodies know before we do. Little secrets rolled up
> and slipped in the flutes of our bones. Mystery loves, mystery griefs,
> longings so private that we act on them before we even feel them.
>
> *El Otro* [The Other] (1997)

[Writing about the border] is part of my cultural background. It's part of who I am, having been born and raised there.

El Andar (Winter 1999)

There's a huge Latino (Mexican) population in Chicago. They know what's going on. They know that things are going to happen around the border sometime in the future that's going to blow this country wide open.

El Andar (Winter 1999)

What is it about our prejudice, our biases, our judgment as Americans, that makes us do what we do? That makes us act? Those are the things that are important in my work.

El Andar (Winter 1999)

I think at the heart, all theater is about relationships.

El Andar (Winter 1999)

I have to do research, obviously, in the issues and pathologies that are going to be key in the work that I write. And I do the research. But ultimately the impulses that I have to study and examine are all inside me.

El Andar (Winter 1999)

Sammy Sosa (San Pedro de Macoris, Dominican Republic, 1968)

After only ten years in the major leagues, Sammy Sosa is already one of the greatest sluggers in baseball history. He hit sixty-six home runs and became known as the prince to Mark McGwire's king in the 1998 season. A national hero in his native country, he founded the Sammy Sosa Foundation, a charitable organization. Sosa won the Roberto Clemente Man of the Year Award in 1998.

I was trying to hit two home runs in every at-bat.

New York Times (September 1, 1998)

I'm rooting for [rival] Mark McGwire. I look up to him the way a son does to his father. I look at him, the way he hits, the way he acts, and I see the person and the player I want to be.

New York Times (September 15, 1998)

I'm the man in the Dominican Republic. He's [McGwire's] the man in the United States. That's the way it should be.

New York Times (September 15, 1998)

Gary Soto (Fresno, California, 1952)

Winner of more literary awards than any other Hispanic poet in the United States, Gary Soto grew up among the migrant farm workers of

Sammy Sosa. Photo by Steve Schwab. Courtesy of the National Baseball Hall of Fame Library, Cooperstown, N.Y.

California's San Joaquin Valley. In addition to poetry, he has published short stories, novels and screenplays. Soto is a professor of Chicano Studies and English at the University of California, Berkeley.

> Although we looked healthy, clean in the morning, and polite as only Mexicans can be polite, we had a streak of orneriness that we imagined to be normal play.
>
> Gary Soto, *Living Up the Street* (1985)

> Along with my brother and sister I picked grapes until I was fifteen, before giving up and saying that I'd rather wear old clothes than stoop like a Mexican.
>
> Gary Soto, *Living Up the Street* (1985)

> As a kid I had chopped cotton and picked grapes, so I knew work. I knew the fatigue and the boredom and the feeling that there was a good possibility you might have to do such work for years, if not for a lifetime. In fact, as a kid I imagined a dark fate: To marry Mexican poor, work Mexican hours, and in the end die a Mexican death, broke and in despair.
>
> Gary Soto, *Living Up the Street* (1985)

During the recession [of 1973] I roomed with my brother and I suggested that we try to become vegetarians. My brother looked up from his drawing board and replied: "Aren't we already?"

Gary Soto, *Living Up the Street* (1985)

I spotted one face in particular, a Chicano I recognized from high school, and walked over to say *Órale ese!* [Hey man!] We shook hands, *raza* [Chicano] style, and passed stories back and forth like a beach ball: Our marriages, children, cars, and misplaced friends.

Gary Soto, *Living Up the Street* (1985)

This is one of the things I tell my students. Take your work seriously but not yourselves.

Wolfgang Binder (ed.), *Partial Autobiographies: Interviews with Twenty Chicano Poets* (1985)

Ray Suárez (Brooklyn, New York, 1957)

Puerto Rican by heritage, Rafael Ángel Suárez Jr. has been a correspondent for CNN, a reporter and commentator for ABC and CBS Radio, host of National Public Radio's *Talk of the Nation* and a commentator on Public Television's *The News Hour with Jim Lehrer*. He has won many honors, including the Studs Terkel Award, the Benton Fellowship and the Rubén Salazar Award given by the National Council of La Raza. Suárez is a founding member of the Chicago Association of Hispanic Journalists.

I was fortunate enough to be in grad school during the 1990s, at the University of Chicago. I was older than most of my classmates and a peer of many of my instructors. Both students and instructors were smart, hard-working, almost unremittingly serious, and burning with a dedication to the ideals of the academy. Knowledge was an addiction: Once we had some, we wanted more. The way we got it was through inquiry and toil.

Chronicle of Higher Education (November 3, 1999)

I have spoken to hundreds of people who mourn the loss of a sense of place tied to block, school, and neighborhood church. . . . Many conclude there was no other way for things to end up. I'll insist until the day they're tossing spadefuls of city soil on my casket that we gave up far too easily, driven by a range of forces in the society we did not recognize.

Ray Suárez, *The Old Neighborhood* (1999)

We were among the first Americans. Why are we still strangers? The people you call Latinos, Hispanics, Spanish, wetbacks, illegals, and so on drew their first breath when an infant was yanked, wet and screaming, from his mother's womb nine months after Christopher Columbus and his hungry men alighted from their ships and walked ashore on the outlands of the new hemisphere.

Ray Suárez, *The Old Neighborhood* (1999)

Year after year, in Labor Department surveys Latinos post the highest levels of overall workplace participation of any Americans. Yet they remain disproportionately poor, and drop out of high school at stubbornly high rates.

Ray Suárez, *The Old Neighborhood* (1999)

The world of American Latinos, brought to you courtesy of your late local news, is populated by the hard and tragic young men who believe in little except their need to enforce their code on their block. They live among shuttered factories and empty warehouses. . . . Still strangers, they are products of the lead-poisoned soil of the American city. We ignore them at our own peril.

Ray Suárez, *The Old Neighborhood* (1999)

The American city is a stubborn club fighter, fat lip and all. After a long pounding, the crowd was looking for wobbly knees and a glassy stare. But this pug knows the fight is just half over.

Ray Suárez, *The Old Neighborhood* (1999)

Nicomedes Suárez-Araúz (Santa Ana, Bolivia, 1946)

Born in the Amazonian region of Bolivia, Nicomedes Suárez-Araúz has published many books of poetry, fiction and essays. He is the editor of *Amazonian Literary Review* and is a professor at Smith College.

The historical amnesia of my Amazonian land, motive of fables and myths, gave me the freedom to improvise a linguistic veil to cover my region's historical void. This led me . . . to found Loén, my apocryphal homeland, fruit of my nostalgia for a lost paradise: my infancy and my original home. In that imaginary and real land I close my eyes in order to see, with the eyes of fantasy, the worlds, the people and the things that fascinate me. I consider myself to be Loénian, Amazonian and Bolivian.

Original quotation for this book (August 2001)

Decades of life in the United States have sharpened my affection for the defenseless people of my Amazonian homeland. Literature, although it is a place of luminosity and delight, cannot substitute for the vital contact and the material help that I give, within my possibilities, to my Amazonian compatriots. Although I feel full gratitude for the opportunities that the United States has afforded me, I remain firm in my purpose—perhaps quixotically after three decades in this country, a lovely life with an American spouse and two children—of not becoming a naturalized citizen.

Original quotation for this book (August 2001)

T

Cristina Teuscher (New Rochelle, New York, 1978)

Cristina Teuscher helped the American women win a gold medal in the women's 800-meter freestyle relay in the 1996 Atlanta Games, swimming the fastest 200-meter leg in Olympic history. She brought home three gold medals from the Pan American Games the year before in Argentina, her parents' native country.

> I think I've sacrificed like any other athlete who is in high school. But I'm happy. I don't feel like I've missed out on anything. Because when you think about it, how many kids get to say, "Gee, I'm going to the Olympics?"
>
> *Scholastic Update* (April 12, 1996)

> When you finally get in the [starting] blocks you relax. You know you're ready. There's no more time to dwell on it. You just let yourself go, and it's a great feeling.
>
> *New York Times* (July 14, 1996)

Piri Thomas (New York, New York, 1928)

Born of Puerto Rican parents in Spanish Harlem, John Peter "Piri" Thomas is the author of *Down These Mean Streets* (1969), his autobiography; *Savior, Savior Hold This Hand*, (1972); *Stories from the Barrio* (1978) and other works. He is famous for his dramatic speeches and lectures about his transformation from a gang leader, drug addict and convict into an author and social activist.

> Poverty and denial of dignity warp, embitter and destroy millions of lives.
>
> *Saturday Review* (September 23, 1967)

YEE-AH! Wanna know how many times I've stood on a rooftop and yelled out to anybody: "Hey, World—I am. Hallo, World—this is Piri. That's me. I wanna tell ya I'm here—you bunch of mother-jumpers.

Down These Mean Streets (1967)

I'm a skinny, dark-face, curly-haired, intense Porty-Ree-can. Unsatisfied, hoping, always reaching.

Down These Mean Streets (1967)

Hanging around on the block is a sort of science. You have a lot to do and a lot of nothing to do. In the winter there's dancing, pad combing, movies, and the like. But summer is really the kick. All the blocks are alive, like many-legged cats crawling with fleas. People are all over the place. Stoops are occupied like bleacher sections at a game, and beer flows like there's nothing else to drink. The block musicians pound out gone beats on tin cans and conga drums and bongos. And kids are playing all over the place—on fire escapes, under cars, over cars, in alleys, back yards, hallways.

Down These Mean Streets (1967)

Whether you're right or wrong, as long as you're strong, you're right.

Down These Mean Streets (1967)

"I do" and "I do" and "man and woman" and till death do us in, or something like that, and a raising of a veil and a warm gentle kiss and mucho congratulations and Sis and Don and Tia and La Vieja and her revelations and all made a warmness into a Puerto Rican symphony of getting married sounds.

Savior, Savior Hold My Hand (1972)

To us people of the Barrio, the ghetto is our church, and the only way we're gonna make heaven out of this hell is by getting together.

Savior, Savior Hold My Hand (1972)

Reies López Tijerina (Falls City, Texas, 1926)

An ex-evangelist, Reies Tijerina became one of the most effective land grant activists of the 1960s. He founded the Alianza Federal de Mercedes (Federal Land Grant Alliance) in New Mexico, dedicated to reclaiming historic land grants promised to Mexican Americans by the 1848 Treaty of Guadalupe Hidalgo. Known as "El Tigre del Norte" (Tiger of the North) or "Rey Tigre" (King Tiger), Reies Tijerina is a brilliant speaker who has moved many people to action.

I don't mind the idea of folk hero. Every culture has its needs and its customs.

Qué Nuevas Web site (April 2000)

Reies López Tijerina. Courtesy of the Center for Southwest Research, General Library, University of New Mexico.

Estela Portillo Trambley (El Paso, Texas, 1936)

Estela Portillo Trambley has written plays, short stories and a novel. She won the prestigious Quinto Sol Award for literature in 1973.

> It had been decreed long ago by man-made laws that living things were not equal. It had been decreed that women should be possessions, slaves, pawns in the hands of men with ways of beasts. It had been decreed that women were to be walloped effigies to burn upon the altars of men.
>
> Estela Portillo Trambley, *Rain of Scorpions and Other Writings* (1976)

> Political literature, no matter how clever it might be, tends to make stereotypes of the evil exploiter and the poor, innocent victim. That is not life. The exploiter is a human being too. He might be violent and selfish and greedy and mean, but down deep, despite having mutated into a Machiavellian oddity, he is still human. Once you take this away from your character in literature, you've taken away his life. Political literature assassinates characters.
>
> Juan Bruce-Novoa, *Chicano Authors: Inquiry by Interview* (1980)

Elva Pérez Treviño (San Antonio, Texas)

A third-generation Tejana, author Elva Pérez Treviño has declared that she writes in response to the political implications of being born Mexican in South Texas.

It has been the stark beauty of dark skin Mexicanismo in the landscape and environment that has allowed the magical philosophy of my Raza to survive within me in the form of *el espíritu Mexicano*, luminous source of faith and trust.

Alma Gómez, Cherríe Moraga and Mariana Romo-Carmona (eds.), *Cuentos:
Stories by Latinas* (1983)

There is a certain dignity and sense of self-value knowing my indigenous roots are founded in La Tierra del Sol and the seven tribes of Aztlán. The fiction I compose is inspired by the compassion that has been stirred by other Mexicanos and the women of all nationalities.

Alma Gómez, Cherríe Moraga and Mariana Romo-Carmona (eds.), *Cuentos:
Stories by Latinas* (1983)

Lee Treviño (Dallas, Texas, 1939)

Raised by his mother and grandfather in a farmhouse behind a golf course, Lee Treviño had to drop out of school in the eighth grade to help

Lee Treviño. Courtesy of Assured Management.

his family. He caddied and assisted the club greenskeeper. Later he joined the Marine Corps and represented this branch of the service in golf tournaments. In 1968 Treviño won the U.S. Open, becoming the first player in history to shoot all four rounds below par. In 1971 he was named PGA Player of the Year, AP Athlete of the Year, BBC International Sports Personality of the Year and Sportsman of the Year by *Sports Illustrated.* Treviño has won many other important tournaments and belongs to the World Golf Hall of Fame. Lee Treviño is also known for his philanthropy.

> Fellas, there's a little Mexican boy out in El Paso you're going to have to make room for.
>
> Matt S. Meier, *Notable Latino Americans* (1997)

Félix Trinidad (Cupey Alto, Puerto Rico, 1973)

Known as "Tito" to his friends and fans, boxer Félix Trinidad has enjoyed a sensational career marked by brilliant comebacks. He has been welterweight champion of the world for both the International Boxing Federation and the World Boxing Council.

> I have no doubts about myself.
>
> *Current Biography* (February 2000)

Carmelita Tropicana (Alina Troyano) (Cuba)

Cuban-born Alina Troyano is a writer-actress and performance artist who has won fellowships from the Cintas Foundation and the New York Foundation for the Arts. With Uzi Parnes, she is the author of *I, Carmelita Tropicana*, a compilation of her plays, scripts, essays and other works. With director Ela Troyano, she wrote the script for the movie *Carmelita Tropicana: Your Kunst* [Art] *Is Your Waffen* [War], which won a prize at the 1994 Berlin Film Festival.

> I'm multi-cultural, multi-lingual, multi-sexual, you know, multigenerational, mucho-multi, multi-everything!
>
> *Giant Flip and Fun Carmelita Tropicana Fan Page* Web site (2000)

> Hello people, you know me, I know you. I don't need no American Express card, I am Carmelita Tropicana, superintendent, performance artist.
>
> *I, Carmelita Tropicana* (2000)

> I am an artist, a very, very sensitive person. I suffer a lot from angst. But when I get this angst attack, I turn to the three arts: poetry, macramé, and cooking. Food can elevate, inspire, ennoble.
>
> *I, Carmelita Tropicana* (2000)

Columbus came from strong food cultures, Italy and Spain. He had good food. Why, then, did he come to America? Was he looking for gold? Was he looking for converts to Christianity? No. He was looking for spices. A little pepper and hot sauce to make his Spanish omelet zing with pizzazz.

I, Carmelita Tropicana (2000)

You have to be open. If you close yourself you will succumb to your fears. You may even be dragged down collectively into the muck and mire like the people in California who voted for the anti-immigration legislation, Proposition 187. They had a big fear. Fear of the tortillas. In voting for it they have denied the enrichment that an immigrant group can have on a culture. There is a Yoruba saying [from Nigeria and Benin] for people with food phobias, you are like a fried fish. You have one eye open but you cannot see.

I, Carmelita Tropicana (2000)

I'm like a short-order cook when I make performance art pieces, quickly whipping up a piece for a specific event and audience.

I, Carmelita Tropicana (2000)

Sara Martínez Tucker (Laredo, Texas, 1955)

After working in the private sector, Sara Martínez Tucker was named president and CEO of the National Hispanic Scholarship Fund (NHSF), the country's largest program of its kind.

My parents struggled to give us a college education. . . . Father always talked to us about having a choice in life, and he said an education would give us that choice.

Hispanic (December 1997)

Christy Turlington (Walnut Creek, California, 1969)

Daughter of an American father and a Salvadoran mother, Christy Turlington became a super-model in the late 1980s and early 1990s. She has donated to antismoking campaigns and to causes for the people of El Salvador.

People don't want to like you. You're young and beautiful and successful. They think you don't have a skill. So when things go well for you, they aren't happy. That's human nature.

New York (March 9, 1992)

I'd rather go naked than wear fur.

Advertising campaign for People for the Ethical Treatment of Animals (PETA)
(1995)

U

María-Luisa Urdaneta (Cali, Colombia, 1931)

Feminist María-Luisa Urdaneta is an anthropologist, author, lecturer and women's rights activist. In 1985 she was named to the San Antonio Women's Hall of Fame.

> Our family had always looked at the U.S. as a mecca—a place to fulfill your dreams. Becoming a naturalized citizen was second nature. It was an unbelievable gift.
>
> Joseph M. Palmisano (ed.), *Notable Hispanic American Women*, Book II (1998)

Luis Alberto Urrea (Tijuana, Mexico, 1955)

Born of an Anglo mother and a Mexican father, Luis Alberto Urrea moved with his parents to San Diego at the age of three. He is the author of novels, short stories, essays, poetry and plays and is also a journalist and visual artist. His works relate the compelling story of his life between two parents, two countries and two cultures. Urrea won the Western States Book Award for his book of poems, *The Fever of Being* (1994), and the American Book Award for the last volume of his "border trilogy," *Nobody's Son: Notes from an American Life* (1998).

> My art work is a chronicle of a longing—perhaps for God, perhaps for shelter. Everybody there is looking for home.
>
> *Imagine: International Chicano Poetry Journal* (Summer/Winter 1986)

> It has been estimated that by 2050, Latinos will be the majority population of the world. . . . NASA will land the first lowrider on the moon. Just watch.
>
> *Nobody's Son: Notes from an American Life* (1998)

America—there's a Mexican in the woodpile.

Nobody's Son: Notes from an American Life (1998)

America is home. It's the only home I have. Both Americas. All three Americas, from the Arctic Circle to Tierra del Fuego.

Nobody's Son: Notes from an American Life (1998)

For I am nobody's son. But I am everybody's brother.

Nobody's Son: Notes from an American Life (1998)

There is a way in which a family shares one bathroom that says *love*. There is even a way in which a cup of coffee at three o'clock on a slow and rainy day says *love*.

Nobody's Son: Notes from an American Life (1998)

Most everything I write ends up being tragicomic. Even when I don't mean to, I often write the saddest comedies in town.

Dictionary of Literary Biography: Chicano Writers, Vol. 209 (1999)

Life in our home was an emotional minefield. These are ghosts that haunt me to this day.

Dictionary of Literary Biography: Chicano Writers, Vol. 209 (1999)

V

Luis Valdez (Delano, California, 1940)

Known as the father of Chicano theater, Luis Valdez has distinguished himself as an actor, director, playwright, producer and filmmaker. With the creation of Teatro Campesino, he brought his artistic skills to the aid of labor activist César Chávez and the farm workers in the grape strike in his hometown of Delano. Valdez wrote the screenplays for the films *Zoot Suit* (1981) and *La Bamba* (1989), a movie that he also directed.

> Art is not a question of affirmative action. It is an affirmation of one's belief in human universality.
>
> Luis Reyes and Peter Rubie, *Hispanics in Hollywood* (1994)

> I will not be intimidated into making my vision of American coincide with whatever is politically correct at the moment. I have helped to define the Latino identity in America through my plays and films, but I will not be coerced into limiting my artistic choices in violation of basic human principles.
>
> Luis Reyes and Peter Rubie, *Hispanics in Hollywood* (1994)

> My social objective has always been to counteract racism in the world, not reinforce it.
>
> Luis Reyes and Peter Rubie, *Hispanics in Hollywood* (1994)

Patssi Valdez (Los Angeles, California, 1951)

A founding member of the multimedia group Asco, artist Patssi Valdez combines the imagery of her ancestral Mexico with the avant-garde.

Chicana art has all these faces, all these styles. You can create any kind of art you want to be. You don't need to limit yourself. You can open up the umbrella.

Joseph M. Palmisano (ed.), *Notable Hispanic American Women*, Book II (1998)

Fernando Valenzuela (Navajoa, Mexico, 1960)

A colorful left-handed pitcher who took the baseball world by storm in his first season with the Los Angeles Dodgers, Fernando Valenzuela was named Rookie of the Year and the *Sporting News* Major League Player of the Year in 1981. "Fernandomania" hit southern California. Valenzuela won the Cy Young and the Golden Glove Awards. He was named to the National League All-Star team five times and played in five championship games and in two world series. He still plays professional baseball in Mexico.

Fernando Valenzuela. Courtesy of the National Baseball Hall of Fame Library, Cooperstown, N.Y.

[On his famous silences] I understand more than people think. . . . I don't say anything only because I can't speak English.

Los Angeles Times (May 1, 1981)

The cheers keep me going. This [pitching] allows me to give something to the people, whatever I have left, in return for all the support they have given me.

Baseball Digest (July 2001)

To keep going in baseball, you have to learn all the time. I love to play. When I can't get outs, I'll stop.

Baseball Digest (July 2001)

Gloria Vando (Hickok) (New York, New York, 1936)

Grandniece of the famous Spanish composer Enrique Granados and daughter of a well-known night club performer, Gloria Vando is a poet whose work evokes her experience of growing up Puerto Rican in New York. She is also an editor.

I have straddled the fine line of *patria* [homeland] all my life: a Yankee in Puerto Rico and a Latina in the States; a part of each world and apart from each world. I grew up dancing to Agustín Lara and Frank Sinatra, eating *tostones* [fried plantains] and apple pie, and speaking Spanish and English. As a writer I could be rooted in and inspired by the classical tradition, but I had the freedom—indeed, the obligation—to nurture my own bilingual voice.

Original quotation for this book (February 2001)

To be a Latino writer and not be political is to be impervious to the needs of your people—and as a Latino writer, you soon learn that all suffering people are your people.

Original quotation for this book (February 2001)

Here in the States we are told about and concern ourselves with human rights in China, South Africa, Central America, Bosnia, and Afghanistan, but we are kept ignorant of what is going on in our own backyard— Puerto Rico.

Original quotation for this book (February 2001)

Since we live in a world that is doing its best to *cortarnos con la misma tijera* (cut us with the same scissor), it is important to nurture and celebrate what is distinctive in each of us. By exploring our uniqueness, we will inevitably uncover how much we have in common.

Original quotation for this book (February 2001)

My mother's advice to me and my advice to my children: "When going out in the world, wear your emotional overcoat."

Original quotation for this book (February 2001)

Language is power. Indeed, language for me has always been a source of power—and freedom, they seem to go hand in hand. Language opens up possibilities, expands choices, enables one to dream and hope. Words are the stepping stones out of the ghetto, out of the imprisoned self.

Original quotation for this book (February 2001)

Wordplay gives one a heightened awareness of language, and a freedom unavailable in any other form—refracted, prismatic, offering infinite possibilities of nuance and color. An exiled language takes on an added dimension—it is understood on two levels, the original and what it has become in its new environment. Like those who speak it, the language subsequently assumes a new national identity. It becomes rich in irony.

Original quotation for this book (February 2001)

Diana L. Vargas (Bronx, New York, 1961)

Diana L. Vargas is vice-president and general manager of the second-largest television market in the nation, KTTV/FOX 11 in Los Angeles.

Even when I was very little I read volumes and volumes of books. I also loved to write because writing allowed my imagination to take me any-where. It was a form of expression and escape.

Joseph M. Palmisano (ed.), *Notable Hispanic American Women*, Book II (1998)

Elizabeth Vargas (ca. 1963)

After studying journalism at the University of Missouri, Elizabeth Vargas began her career as a television news correspondent and later became host of major network programs such as *Good Morning America, 20/20* and *Prime Time Live*. She has also been an anchor on *World News Tonight Saturday*.

Nothing compares to the impact of television on the lives of the public.

Joseph M. Palmisano (ed.), *Notable Hispanic American Women*, Book II (1998)

Mario Vargas Llosa (Arequipa, Peru, 1936)

Although he has spent most of his life in his native Peru and in Europe, writer Mario Vargas Llosa's parents lived in Los Angeles for many years, and his son has also resided in the *United States*. He has taught at several American universities. Vargas Llosa is recognized as one of the greatest living novelists in Spanish.

I see in California, and especially in Los Angeles, a mirror of the coming millennium, of a future in which, let us hope, human beings may move through the wide world as if at home, crossing and recrossing frontiers that will have faded to the point of pointlessness, living and mixing with men and women of other languages, races and creeds, putting down roots wherever they please . . . materializing that right to happiness which the Constitution of the United States—alone in the world, so far as I know—grants to its citizens.

El Andar (Winter 1999)

Among the many tributaries of this great river of immigration, that from Latin America has been the most numerous and constant, giving an unmistakable color and flavor to the state of California and to this city [Los Angeles].

El Andar (Winter 1999)

Nobody who speaks and writes Spanish can feel like an outsider in a city [Los Angeles] so impregnated with Latin American culture. My parents' case is that of countless families or individuals who, coming from all corners of the world, through hard work found here the encouragement to live and work which, for economic and political reasons or both, their countries of origin denied to them.

El Andar (Winter 1999)

Enedina Casárez Vásquez (San Antonio, Texas, 1945)

The daughter of migrant workers, Enedina Casárez Vásquez creates *nichos*, or miniature box altars, a disappearing art in Mexican American life.

The *nichos* [miniature box altars] perpetuate a need to reach out and share dreams and hopes with people.

Joseph M. Palmisano (ed.), *Notable Hispanic American Women*, Book II (1998)

Ed Vega (Ponce, Puerto Rico, 1936)

After graduating from New York University, writer Edgardo "Ed" Vega Yunqué did social work and taught at several universities. He is the author of *The Comeback* (1985), a satire of ethnic autobiography and the identity crisis, as embodied in a half-Puerto Rican, half-Eskimo ice hockey player. Vega's other works include *Mendoza's Dreams* (1987) and *Casualty Report* (1991). He was awarded a National Endowment for the Arts fellowship in 1989 and a New York Foundation for the Arts grant in 1990.

It is . . . repulsive for me to write an autobiographical novel about being an immigrant. In fact, I don't like ethnic literature, except when the language is so good that you forget about the ethnic writing in it.

The Comeback (1985)

Patricia Velásquez (Maracaibo, Venezuela)

A super-model turned actress, Patricia Velásquez has starred in several Hollywood movies.

> I believe that when the universe gives you something, you have to give in return. If it's all about you, the universe will take it back.
>
> *Latina* (May 2000)

Nydia Velázquez (Yabucoa, Puerto Rico, 1953)

Daughter of a sugarcane cutter, Nydia Margarita Velázquez became the first Puerto Rican woman to be elected to the U.S. Congress. She has established herself as an advocate for Hispanics, women, immigrants and the working class. She has sat on important committees in the House and was former director of the Department of Puerto Rican Community Affairs in the United States.

Congresswoman Nydia Velázquez. Courtesy of the U.S. House of Representatives.

I am very clear: I am not going to represent only a Puerto Rican or a Latin American viewpoint. I have a very wide perspective.

New York Times (September 27, 1992)

If I do not get something I want today, I will come back tomorrow and tomorrow until they get tired of seeing me.

New York Times (September 27, 1992)

They might dilute Latinos in the [congressional] district, but not their voting power. What is true of minorities is that we are not in power, we're not in control of the legislative process. But that does not mean we are not fighting back.

Hispanic (October 1995)

My thing has always been to help my community to help themselves, to make them self-sufficient. One area that is important is economic development to create jobs because we need to revitalize our neighborhoods. Education is [also] a key element for a poor community.

Hispanic (October 1995)

Lauren Vélez (Brooklyn, New York)

After ten years in theater, actress Lauren Vélez broke into film and television. She is best known for her role as the smart, tough detective Nina Moreno on Fox Television's hit show *New York Undercover*.

I get a lot of young Latino girls who say to me "It's so nice to finally see a person on TV who looks like me."

People Weekly (January 20, 1997)

Lisa Vélez (New York, New York, 1967)

The youngest of ten children, Lisa Vélez was raised in the neighborhood of Manhattan known as Hell's Kitchen. "Lisa Lisa" became a popular singer as a teenager and recorded several Top 40 hits.

Step back and watch out! I want to bring the Puerto Ricans out. Boom!

Time (July 11, 1988)

Anita Vélez-Mitchell (Vieques, Puerto Rico, 1922)

Dancer, choreographer, stage director, journalist, writer and poet, Anita Vélez-Mitchell has published essays, short stories and poems in leading journals in both English and Spanish. Her book *Primavida* (1986) was awarded Puerto Rico's Julia de Burgos Poetry Prize. She has also been named Poet of the Year by the Institute of Puerto Rico in New York, and Woman of the Year 2000 by the National Conference of Puerto Rican

Women in the United States. A documentary film, *Anita Vélez: Dancing through Life* (2000) is based on her life.

Acting is a re-creation by a few of a creation by one to re-create the many whether it be in theater or in real life.

Original quotation for this book (March 2001)

Had I known life to ebb so swiftly I would have given a tremendous importance to time, giving every heartbeat to the bettering of my understanding of life and consequently of myself.

Original quotation for this book (March 2001)

Each one of us is a unique creation. There is not a person in the world who is exactly like me. I am one and only, a unique sample of the human race.

Original quotation for this book (March 2001)

Meritocracy is important for a democracy.

Original quotation for this book (March 2001)

There is something beyond ourselves that one tacitly feels but does not know yet, it leads us on.

Original quotation for this book (March 2001)

If one's ambitions are overdemanding, one is aware of only the negative side of life, and even of oneself.

Original quotation for this book (March 2001)

The second cup of coffee can never surpass the satisfaction that the first one brings—and in love the first quench is summer and the second, spring.

Original quotation for this book (March 2001)

Happiness is a question one has to answer oneself.

Original quotation for this book (March 2001)

The Angel of Love with his arrow pierces the naughty devil. . . . But the Devil never dies, and bit by bit with his fork the Devil will eat our hearts out and force the Angel of Love to fly.

Original quotation for this book (March 2001)

A scheming person will doubt everyone else's actions.

Original quotation for this book (March 2001)

Taxes are the supreme sacrifice one pays for penny-pinching.

Original quotation for this book (March 2001)

In the fusion of two contradictory opinions shines the truth.

Original quotation for this book (March 2001)

How can I not be happy if at my age I still have ten fingers, ten toes and the tip of my nose!

Original quotation for this book (March 2001)

The gesture cannot afford the luxury of repentance.
> Original quotation for this book (March 2001)

Know the truth so you can tell the most convincing lie.
> Original quotation for this book (March 2001)

Those who do not believe in some sort of resurrection can only believe in death (therefore the happy ending).
> Original quotation for this book (March 2001)

When you come to laugh at love, love already has been laughing itself to death.
> Original quotation for this book (March 2001)

Western civilization has come to comprehend the universe, and the mystic East has come to comprehend man. It is time that East and West be one. (Versus East is East and West is West and never the twain shall meet.)
> Original quotation for this book (March 2001)

Carmelita Vigil-Schimmenti (Albuquerque, New Mexico, 1936)

In 1985, Brigadier General Carmelita Vigil-Schimmenti, U.S. Air Force, became the first Hispanic woman to attain the rank of general in the American armed forces. She traces her family's origins in New Mexico to 1695.

> I worked very hard. I had the advantage of having grown up with parents who taught me that when committing yourself to an employer, you give them your best. And so, I went into the military with a good philosophy and work ethic that I thank my parents for.
> Rose Díaz, *Nuestras Mujeres: Hispanas of New Mexico* (1992)

Lydia Villa-Komaroff (Las Vegas, New Mexico, 1947)

When she received her Ph.D. in cell biology from the Massachusetts Institute of Technology in 1975, Lydia Villa-Komaroff was only the third Mexican American woman in the United States to earn a doctorate in the sciences. She went on to teach and do research. She has served as vice-president for research and graduate studies at Northwestern University. Villa-Komaroff is a founding member of the Society for the Advancement of Chicanos and Native Americans in Science.

> There is not a child in the world, I don't think, who doesn't begin as a scientist.
> Speech for the National Science Foundation (1995)

In the southwestern Chicano culture that I came from, many parents, consciously or unconsciously, discourage children from pursuing higher education because they are afraid that education will change their children or that the children will be lost to them. I think it's incumbent on people like me to convince parents that they won't lose their child to education, but that it will enrich the child and thus the family.

Susan A. Ambrose and others, *Journeys of Women in Science and Engineering: No Universal Constraints* (1997)

I learned early on that it's a very good ploy to act confident even when you're not because then people perceive you as confident, and that makes a big difference.

Susan A. Ambrose and others, *Journeys of Women in Science and Engineering: No Universal Constraints* (1997)

Alma Luz Villanueva (Lompoc, California, 1944)

A writer of Mexican, Yaqui (Native American) and German descent, Alma Villanueva has been a writer-in-residence at Stanford University and the University of California at Irvine and at Santa Cruz. She is the author of six volumes of poetry and the winner of an American Book Award for her novel *Ultraviolet Sky* (1989). Her novel *Naked Ladies* won the Josephine Miles PEN Fiction Award (1994) and her poetry collection *Planet* won the Latin American Writers Institute Award in the same year.

Though I *love* California, where I was born, lived for 55 years—I'm realizing the inherent racism I dealt with daily, my name suggesting I could be an "illegal alien." Here in New Mexico I feel "recognized" as the *mestiza* (Yaqui, Mexican, white) I am—people say my name right. The feeling is white people are the *guests* here, taking part in the Indian-Mexican culture. Spanish is spoken loudly in public places—often accompanied by loud laughter—in short, the tone of the Indian-Mexican people is undefeated—I'm enjoying it immensely.

Original quotation for this book (November 2000)

I pay $10 to enter Taos Pueblo,
1,000 year old Earth
homes—I stand in
the center of a
circle, the spirits
pass through me clear
as wind water clouds rain—
a young man welcomes
me, a woman my age greets
me, a man selling jewelry has
my grandmother's maiden name,
LUJÁN (on a sign), yet it all feels
dead, staged, until I
come to a singing

Alma Luz Villanueva. Photo by Leon Canerot. Courtesy of Ms. Villanueva.

creek . . . a young boy
(who looks like my son
at that age) smiles as his
dog rolls in the cool
water on a hot day, "He
likes the water," the boy
laughs, "I don't blame
him," I laugh back . . .
the sign says, "Don't
pet the animals" as the dog
follows me, I pet his wet nose—
I follow a dirt trail, sit by
the singing creek, a sign

says "Stay out of water" . . .
I just rest my eyes on it.
A grandfather speaks to his
horse behind me in Tiwa,
a language never to be
written or recorded, I'm
told, the language sounds
like wind water clouds rain
child's laughter . . .
As I stand to leave,
I see a bright
2pm sun, bleached white
pristine men's underwear
on a hanger by
itself—I wonder if a
tourist took a photo of
real Indian underwear,
I laugh softly
and leave as I can
not bring myself to buy (or sell)
the wind I breathe (this moment).

To my ancestors, Yaqui to Pueblo
Taos Pueblo, New Mexico
Original poem for this book (August 2000)

Tino Villanueva (San Marcos, Texas, 1941)

The founder of Imagine Publishers and *Imagine: International Chicano Poetry Journal*, Tino Villanueva has taught at Boston University.

> I remember my mother would say such things as, "Don't get your
> clothes too dirty, because we don't want the Anglos to think that the
> Mexican is a dirty person."
>
> Wolfgang Binder (ed.), *Partial Autobiographies: Interviews with Twenty Chicano
> Poets* (1985)

José Antonio Villarreal (Los Angeles, California, 1924)

Best known for his novel *Pocho* (1959), José Antonio Villarreal has led a
wandering life that has led him from California to Mexico and back again.

> Regarding the breakdown of the family unit . . . no one could be blamed,
> for the transition from the culture of the old world to that of the new
> should never have been attempted in one generation. Today, in many
> cases, succeeding generations have made a successful transition . . . not
> without some degree of cultural and linguistic loss.
>
> Original quotation for this book (June 2000)

José Antonio Villarreal. Photo by Michael Elderman. Courtesy of Mr. Villarreal.

Víctor Villaseñor (Carlsbad, California, 1940)

Author of the popular *Rain of Gold* (1991) and the screenplay for the award-winning *Ballad of Gregorio Cortez* (1983), Víctor Villaseñor lives on the ranch where he grew up in San Diego County.

And so her heart was ready to break again but then, to her surprise, each new peril only showed her a deeper mystery in this dream called life, *la vida*.

Rain of Gold (1991)

Even God needs help.

Rain of Gold (1991)

It never failed to amaze him how different his people were from the Anglos. *Los mejicanos* never wasted anything. Instead of green grass in front of their homes, they had vegetable gardens. And they didn't fence in their livestock, but let them roam free so they could eat anything they could find. Instead, they fenced in their crops.

Rain of Gold (1991)

"Smart ideas are a dime a dozen, unless you figure out all the thousands of little details that give life to an idea so that the idea can survive."

Rain of Gold (1991)

Then in the distance, Lupe saw the sea and was filled with a wonderful feeling; a much kinder God lived there.

Rain of Gold (1991)

It felt good to talk to his old Friend, God, and have love in his heart.

Rain of Gold (1991)

Helena María Viramontes (East Los Angeles, California, 1954)

Born into an urban family of eleven, Helena María Viramontes has received popular and critical acclaim for her short stories and novels. She was the first Latina to win the prestigious John Dos Passos Award for

Helena María Viramontes. Courtesy of Arte Público Press.

literature (1995). She has also been a community organizer and coordinator of the Los Angeles Latino Writers Association. Viramontes and her husband, the biologist Eloy Rodríguez, consider themselves healers of the body and the soul, warriors for their "community called the universe." Both are professors at Cornell University.

> When I think about the journey to get a novel completed, I can't help but recall all those people throughout the years that have influenced and helped me. It's amazing to remember the times I wrote with Pilar strapped to my back or nursed Francisco while typing.
>
> Helena María Viramontes, Acknowledgments, *Under the Feet of Jesus* (1995)

> Now I look at my lovely son and beautiful daughter and I wonder where I tucked away all this thing called time.
>
> Helena María Viramontes, Acknowledgments, *Under the Feet of Jesus* (1995)

> We did it. This novel I offer to all of you.
>
> Helena María Viramontes, Acknowledgments, *Under the Feet of Jesus* (1995)

> We consider our work an offering to our children.
>
> *Latino* Web site (1997)

> If my mother showed all that is good in being female, my father showed all that is bad in being male.
>
> *Voices from the Gaps* Web site (1999)

> I didn't pull myself up by the bootstraps, I had a lot of help from my family.
>
> *Rodríguez Latinolink* Web site (2000)

Carmen Delgado Votaw (Humacao, Puerto Rico, 1935)

After a long career as a human and women's rights activist, Carmen Delgado Votaw was named director of government relations for United Way of America. She has received the National Hispanic Heritage Award for education.

> Growing up, we were expected to do something for others. An old lady in our town who lived alone was simply expected at our house every lunch time, and we children were expected to have lunch out for her. We had to be kind to all old folk and talk to lonely people. My father would ask, "Did you stop and talk to Mama Lola today?" And the whole town was my keeper. If I was where I shouldn't be, people would go to my home and say: "Do you know where Carmencita is . . . ?" Growing up like that you know who you are—know you are important.
>
> Joseph M. Palmisano (ed.), *Notable Hispanic American Women*, Book II (1998)

W

Raquel Welch (Chicago, Illinois, 1940)

Born Raquel Tejada to an American mother and a Bolivian father, her early films established her as a sex symbol, an image she has shaken in her later films. She won a Golden Globe Award for best actress in *The Four Musketeers* (1975). In 1990 she was named Woman of the Year by the Los Angeles Hispanic Women's Council.

> All I ever fought for was quality in my films. I really felt I was being penalized for being the sex symbol they had created, and that made my Spanish blood boil.
>
> *Hispanic* (April 1988)

> I've won my stripes. . . . I've gone from just being a sex symbol to being thought of as a legitimate actress.
>
> *Hispanic* (April 1988)

> I've always thought the older I get the more people would see that I have more to me than just my good looks.
>
> *Hispanic* (April 1988)

> You should never give up in life. . . . You have to struggle for something and always think that the best is still to come.
>
> *Cristina* (October 2000)

> I think it's great to [immigrate] here because of the American dream, but not to cut off the roots of what is real and what is your heritage.
>
> *Cigar Aficionado* (August 2001)

> It's funny, but when you're not paying attention and not looking for love is when it happens.
>
> *Cigar Aficionado* (August 2001)

If you take an oak tree and you hit it with lightning, it's going to crack and break. But the reed, it flows back and forth in the wind and keeps coming back up. And that is the thing about me—I always come back up.

Cigar Aficionado (August 2001)

I mean, I've fulfilled almost everybody else's fantasy all these years, so now it's time for my own.

Cigar Aficionado (August 2001)

Vanna White (Conway, South Carolina, 1957)

The long-running, syndicated television game show *Wheel of Fortune* has made its cohost, Vanna White, a well-known personality in the United States and abroad.

> Motherhood has changed my whole attitude about a career. Being a mother is the most important thing.
>
> Joseph M. Palmisano (ed.), *Notable Hispanic American Women*, Book II (1998)

William Carlos Williams (Rutherford, New Jersey, 1883–1963)

Son of an American father and a Puerto Rican mother, William Carlos Williams was a practicing physician for over 50 years who became one of the most important poets in the modernist movement in America. His most well-known work of poetry is *Paterson* (1963). Williams also wrote novels and essays, including *In the American Grain* (1925). He was awarded the Pulitzer Prize for poetry posthumously in 1963. William Carlos Williams always showed a particular interest in Hispanic literature and culture.

> [Speaking of another poet] It isn't what he says that counts as a work of art, it's what he makes with such intensity of perception that it lives with an intrinsic movement of its very own to verify the authenticity.
>
> *The Later Collected Poems of William Carlos Williams* (1950)

Y

Lea Ybarra (Unknown place and date of birth)

A university professor and administrator, Lea Ybarra has been named Hispanic Educator of the Year and received, among others, the Rosa Parks Award for Outstanding Community Service. She is currently executive director of the Institute for the Academic Advancement for Youth at Johns Hopkins University.

> The very soul of the Latino experience is rooted in the family. *La familia* defines our experience at the moment of conception and throughout our lives, and also shapes our identity.
>
> Edward James Olmos, Lea Ybarra and Manuel Monterrey, *Americanos: Latino Life in the United States* (1999)

> A discussion of the Latino family is incomplete without recognition of the central role Latina women have played in both the family and the community. Despite the stereotypical portrayal of Latinas as passive women, they have always been a source of strength for family members. They maintain and nurture strong familial ties and loyalty.... As grandmothers, mothers, and daughters, single, divorced, or married, they are the cornerstones of family life.
>
> Edward James Olmos, Lea Ybarra and Manuel Monterrey, *Americanos: Latino Life in the United States* (1999)

Z

Bernice Zamora (Aguilar, Colorado, 1938)

A seminal poet in the Chicano movement, Bernice Zamora teaches Latino, Native American and contemporary American literature.

> [When asked about her ancestry] It is difficult for me to speak about this because I feel that tracing one's genealogy is an exercise in arrogance. It paves the way for unwarranted vanity on the one hand, and/or defensiveness on the other.
>
> Wolfgang Binder (ed.), *Partial Autobiographies: Interviews with Twenty Chicano Poets* (1985)

APPENDIX I

Anonymous Graffiti, Quotations and Proverbs

The Hispanic oral tradition remains very strong in the United States. For this reason we have created this appendix with a brief selection of anonymous sayings. Although some have equivalents in English and other languages, others are virtually untranslatable. In addition to proverbs and other expressions, the Hispanic oral tradition includes folktales, jokes and ballads, which are beyond the scope of this anthology.

A caballo regalado no se le mira el diente [colmillo] [Don't look a gift horse in the mouth].

Agua que no has de beber, déjala correr [If you're not going to drink the water, let it flow].

Al que madruga Dios le ayuda [The early bird catches the worm, *or* God helps the man who helps himself].

Aunque la mona se vista de seda, mona se queda [You can't make a silk purse out of a sow's ear].

Camarón que se duerme, se lo lleva la corriente [Time and tide wait for no man (woman)].

"C/S" [*Con safos* = "protected by God" or "same to you if you touch this"].

Often seen in Chicano gang graffiti, especially in the 1960s and 1970s

Cuando el río suena, agua lleva [trae] [Where there's smoke, there's fire].

De músico, poeta y loco todos tenemos un poco [We all have a little bit of the musician, the poet and the crazy person].

De tal palo, tal astilla [A chip off the old block].

Dime con quién andas y te diré quién eres [You can tell a man (woman) by the company he (she) keeps].

El que con lobos anda, a aullar se enseña [He (she) that lies with dogs, rises with fleas].

El que mucho abarca, poco aprieta [Don't bite off more than you can chew].

El sol sale para pobres y ricos [The sun rises for rich and poor alike].

En boca cerrada no entran moscas [If you keep your mouth shut, you won't get in trouble, *or* Silence is golden].

En casa del herrero, cuchillo [azada] de palo [In the cobbler's house, the children go unshod, *or* Who is worse shod than the shoemaker's wife?].

Más sabe el diablo por viejo que por diablo [Experience is the best teacher].

Más vale pájaro en mano que cien volando [A bird in hand is worth two in the bush].

Más vale tarde que nunca [Better late than never].

No hay mal que por bien no venga [Every cloud has a silver lining].

No por mucho madrugar amanece más temprano [Everything at its appointed time].

Ojos que no ven, corazón que no siente [Out of sight, out of mind].

Perro que ladra no muerde [His (her) bark is worse than his (her) bite].

"P/V" [*Por vida* = for life, forever].

Often seen in Chicano gang graffiti

Rifamos [We rule].

Often seen in Chicano gang graffiti

Vida loca [Crazy life].

Often seen in Chicano gang graffiti

Viva la Raza Cósmica [Long live the cosmic race or people].

Sometimes seen in Chicano gang graffiti

APPENDIX II
Fields of Professional Activity

Actor/Actress

Acevedo, Kirk
Alba, Jessica
Anthony, Marc
Arnaz, Desi
Arnaz, Lucie
Banderas, Antonio
Bardem, Javier
Blades, Rubén
Carey, Mariah
Carter, Lynda
Colón, Miriam
Cruz, Penélope
del Río, Dolores
Díaz, Cameron
Elizondo, Héctor
Estrada, Erik
Ferrer, José
Fuentes, Daisy
García, Andy
Guzmán, Luis
Hayek, Salma
Hayworth, Rita
Julia, Raúl
Jurado, Katy
Leguizamo, John

López, Jennifer
Manzano, Sonia
Marie, Constance
Marín, Richard "Cheech"
Martín, Ricky
Móntez, María
Moreno, Rita
Olmos, Edward James
Peña, Elizabeth
Pérez, Rosie
Quinn, Anthony
Ravera, Gina
Rivera, Chita
Rodríguez, Paul
Romero, César
Sheen, Martin (Ramón Estévez)
Smits, Jimmy
Solís, Octavio
Tropicana, Carmelita (Alina Troyano)
Valdez, Luis
Velásquez, Patricia
Vélez, Lauren
Welch, Raquel

Airforce Academy Graduate

Cubero, Linda García

Ambassador

Richardson, Bill

Anthropologist

Castaneda, Carlos
Urdaneta, María-Luisa

Archbishop

Flores, Patrick

Architect

Ambasz, Emilio

Artist

Baca, Judith F.
de Hoyos, Ángela
Fuentes, Tina Guerrero
Hernández, Ester
Lichacz, Sheila
López, Yolanda

Mohr, Nicholasa
Roche-Rabell, Arnaldo
Serrano, Andrés
Urrea, Luis Alberto
Valdez, Patssi

Astronaut

Chang-Díaz, Franklin
Ochoa, Ellen

Astrophysicist

Córdova, France Anne

Athlete

Alou, Felipe
Araguz, Leo
Bonilla, Bobby
Campos, Jorge
Canseco, José
Carillo, Mary
Casals, Rosemary
Cepeda, Orlando
Clemente, Roberto

de la Hoya, Óscar
Fernández, Lisa
Fernández, Mary Joe
Galarraga, Andrés
Galindo, Rudy
García, Sergio
Garciaparra, Nomar
Gómez, Lefty (Vernon Louis)
González, Corky (Rodolfo)

Gonzales, Pancho (Richard)
Hernandez, Orlando "El Duque"
Lobo, Rebecca
López, Felipe
López, Luis
López, Nancy
Martínez, Pedro
Mota, Manny
Peña, Carlos
Pérez, Tony

Pincay Jr., Laffit
Piniella, Lou
Rodríguez, Alex
Rodríguez, Chi-Chi
Segura, Pancho
Sosa, Sammy
Teuscher, Cristina
Treviño, Lee
Trinidad, Félix
Valenzuela, Fernando

Author

Agosín, Marjorie
Alfaro, Luis
Allende, Isabel
Álvarez, Julia
Anaya, Rudolfo A.
Anzaldúa, Gloria
Arias, Arturo
Arrarás, María Celeste
Baca, Jimmy Santiago
Benítez, Rubén
Benítez, Sandra
Borinsky, Alicia
Campo, Rafael
Casal, Lourdes
Castaneda, Carlos
Castedo, Elena
Castillo, Ana
Chávez, Denise
Chávez, Linda
Cofer, Judith Ortiz
Cruz, Humberto
Díaz, Junot
Dos Passos, John
Elizondo, Virgilio
Estés, Clarissa Pinkola
Ferré, Rosario
Fuentes, Carlos
García, Cristina
García, Eric
García, Guy
Gilb, Dagoberto

Gómez-Peña, Guillermo
Gonzales, Rodolfo Corky
Gonzales, Sylvia Alicia
Hernández-Ávila, Inés
Hinojosa-Smith, Rolando
Jiménez, Francisco
Lacayo, Richard
López, Barry
Manguel, Alberto
Manzano, Sonia
Martín, Patricia Preciado
Mohr, Nicholasa
Nieto, Sonia M.
Paredes, Américo
Perera, Hilda
Pérez Firmat, Gustavo
Quiñónez, Ernesto
Quintero, Sofía
Rivera, Tomás
Rodríguez, Richard
Santayana, George
Santí, Enrico Mario
Santiago, Esmeralda
Schomberg, Arthur Alfonso
Soto, Gary
Suárez-Araúz, Nicomedes
Thomas, Piri
Trambley, Estela Portillo
Treviño, Elva Pérez
Tropicana, Carmelita (Alina
  Troyano)

Urdaneta, María-Luisa
Urrea, Luis Alberto
Vargas Llosa, Mario
Vega, Ed
Vélez-Mitchell, Anita

Villanueva, Alma Luz
Villarreal, José Antonio
Villaseñor, Víctor
Viramontes, Helena María

Business Leader

Barajas, Louis
Chávez-Thompson, Linda
Goizueta, Robert
Martines, Julie A.

Ortega, Katherine D.
Roque, Margarita
Tucker, Sara Martínez
Vargas, Diana L.

Cellist

Casals, Pablo

Choreographer

Limón, José
Pérez, Rosie
Vélez-Mitchell, Anita

Cinematographer

Almendros, Néstor

Comedian/Comedienne

Charo (María Pilar Martínez)
Guerra, Jackie
Leguizamo, John
Marín, Richard "Cheech"

Ortelli, Dyana
Quintero, Sofía
Rodríguez, Paul

Community Organizer

Alfaro, Luis
Gonzales, Mary
Gonzales, Rodolfo Corky

Rodríguez, Eloy
Roque, Margarita
Viramontes, Helena María

Composer

Arnaz, Desi
Blades, Rubén
Casals, Pablo
Charo (María Pilar Martínez)
Guerrero, Lalo

Iglesias, Enrique
León, Tania
Puente, Tito
Santana, Carlos

Conductor

Casals, Pablo
León, Tania

Congressman/Congresswoman

Bonilla, Henry
González, Henry B.
Montoya, Joseph M.
Peña, Federico F.
Rangel, Charles B.

Richardson, Bill
Ros-Lehtinen, Ileana
Roybal, Edward R.
Roybal-Allard, Lucille
Velázquez, Nydia

Curator

Alfaro, Luis
Schomburg, Arthur Alfonso
Sandoval, Denise

Dancer

Charo (María Pilar Martínez)
Corella, Ángel
Herrera, Paloma
Limón, José

López, Lourdes
Moreno, Rita
Rivera, Chita
Vélez-Mitchell, Anita

Director

Alfaro, Luis
Arnaz, Desi
Colón, Miriam
García, Andy
Machado, Eduardo
Marín, Richard "Cheech"
Nava, Gregory

Olmos, Edward James
Quintero, José
Rodríguez, Robert
Solís, Octavio
Valdez, Luis
Vélez-Mitchell, Anita

Ecologist

López, Barry

Economist

Gillespie, Arlene F.

Editor

de Hoyos, Ángela
Guzmán, Sandra
Manguel, Albert
Martínez, Silvia A.

Moraga, Cherríe
Rebolledo, Tey Diana
Vando (Hickoc), Gloria

Educator

Alvarado, Anthony
Álvarez, Julia
Chávez, Linda
Fernández, Celestino
Gonzales, Sylvia Alicia

Jiménez, Francisco
Mateu, Milagros
Mora, Pat
Rivera, Tomás
Villa-Komaroff, Lydia

Entrepreneur

Vásquez, Enedina Casárez
Villanueva, Tino

Fashion Designer

de la Renta, Óscar
Herrera, Carolina
Picasso, Paloma

Fashion Model

Fuentes, Daisy
Turlington, Christy

Folklorist

Paredes, Américo

General

Vigil-Schimmenti, Carmelita

Governor

Ferré, Luis
Richardson, Bill

Humanitarian

Casals, Pablo
Goizueta, Roberto
Julia, Raúl

Industrialist

Ferré, Luis

Inventor

Ambasz, Emilio

Jewelry Designer

Picasso, Paloma

Journalist

Arrarás, María Celeste
García, Guy
Gonzales, Rebecca
Guzmán, Sandra
Hinojosa, María

Martínez, Rubén
Rivera, Geraldo
Suárez, Ray
Vélez-Mitchell, Anita

Labor Leader

Chávez, César
Chávez-Thompson, Linda

Huerta, Dolores
Rodríguez, Arturo

Law Clerk

Cruz, Ted

Lawyer

Peña, Federico F.

Librarian

Martínez, Elizabeth

Military Career

Cubero, Linda García
Vigil-Schimmenti, Carmelita

Musician

Arnaz, Desi
Estefan Jr., Emilio
García, Jerry
Guerrero, Lalo
Iturbi, Amparo
Iturbi, José

Los Lobos (David Hidalgo,
    Conrad Lozano, Louie Pérez,
    César Rojas)
Puente, Tito
Sandoval, Arturo
Santana, Carlos

News Anchor/Correspondent

Arrarás, María Celeste
Collins, María Antonieta
Hinojosa, María

Mora, Antonio
Suárez, Ray
Vargas, Elizabeth

Olympic Medalist

de la Hoya, Óscar
Fernández, Gigi
Fernández, Lisa

Fernández, Mary Joe
Teuscher, Cristina

Performing Artist

Gómez-Peña, Guillermo

Tropicana, Carmelita (Alina
Troyano)

Philanthropist

Ferré, Luis
Goizueta, Roberto

Francisco, Don (Mario
Kreutzberger)
Treviño, Lee

Photographer

Montoya, Linda L.

Physician

Campo, Rafael

Physicist

Báez, Alberto V.

Pianist

Iturbi, Amparo
Iturbi, José

Playwright

Alfaro, Luis
Baca, Jimmy Santiago
López, Josefina
Machado, Eduardo
Moraga, Cherríe
Piñero, Miguel

Rivera, José
Sánchez, Edwin
Solís, Octavio
Tropicana, Carmelita (Alina
Troyano)
Valdez, Luis

Poet

Agosín, Marjorie
Alurista (Alberto Baltazar Urista)
Anzaldúa, Gloria
Baca, Jimmy Santiago
Borinsky, Alicia

Brinson-Pineda, Bárbara
Cervantes, Lorna Dee
Cofer, Judith Ortiz
Corpi, Lucha
Cortés Castaneda, Manuel

Cunningham, Verónica
de Burgos, Julia
de Hoyos, Ángela
Espada, Martín
Galeano, Juan Carlos
Gonzales, Rodolfo Corky
Herrera, Juan Felipe
Martínez, Rubén
Montoya, José
Mora, Pat
Moraga, Cherríe
Paz, Yanira

Salinas, Luis Omar
Salinas, Raúl
Sánchez, Sonia
Santayana, George
Soto, Gary
Urrea, Luis Alberto
Vando (Hickoc), Gloria
Vélez-Mitchell, Anita
Villanueva, Alma Luz
Williams, William Carlos
Zamora, Bernice

Political Commentator

Chávez, Linda

Politician

Bonilla, Henry
Bustamante, Cruz
Cavazos, Lauro F.
Chávez, Dennis
Cisneros, Henry
Crespo, Luigi
Ferré, Luis
Gonzales, Rodolfo Corky
González, Henry B.

Molina, Gloria
Montoya, Joseph M.
Peña, Federico F.
Rangel, Charles B.
Richardson, Bill
Ros-Lehtinen, Ileana
Roybal, Edward R.
Roybal-Allard, Lucille
Velázquez, Nydia

Priest

Cutie, Alberto
Elizondo, Virgilio
Flores, Patrick

Producer

Alfaro, Luis
Arnaz, Desi
Elizondo, Virgilio
García, Andy
Guerrero, Dan
Guzmán, Sandra

Hinojosa, María
Nava, Gregory
Olmos, Edward James
Rodríguez, Robert
Saralegui, Cristina
Valdez, Luis

Professor

Álvarez, Julia
Benítez, Rubén
Betances, Samuel
Borinsky, Alicia
Córdova, France Anne
Cortés Castaneda, Manuel
Elizondo, Virgilio
Galeano, Juan Carlos
Jiménez, Francisco
López, Yolanda
Moreno, Jonathan D.

Paz, Yanira
Pérez-Firmat, Gustavo
Rebolledo, Tey Diana
Ruiz, Vicki
Santí, Enrico Mario
Soto, Gary
Suárez-Araúz, Nicomedes
Urdaneta, María-Luisa
Viramontes, Helena María
Ybarra, Lea

Psychologist

Estés, Clarissa Pinkola

Publisher

de Hoyos, Ángela
Haubegger, Christy
Saralegui, Cristina

Radio-Show Host

Saralegui, Cristina
Suárez, Ray

Scientist

Chang-Díaz, Franklin
Córdova, France Anne
Ocampo, Adriana C.

Rodríguez, Eloy
Villa-Komaroff, Lydia

Screenwriter

Arias, Arturo
Marín, Richard "Cheech"
Nava, Gregory

Tropicana, Carmelita (Alina
  Troyano)
Valdez, Luis
Villaseñor, Víctor

Senator (United States)

Chávez, Dennis
González, Henry B.
Montoya, Joseph M.

Singer

Aguilera, Christina
Anthony, Marc
Arnaz, Desi
Báez, Joan
Blades, Rubén
Carey, Mariah
Carr, Vikki
Charo (María Pilar Martínez)
Cruz, Celia
Domingo, Plácido
Estefan, Gloria
García, Jerry
Hinojosa, Tish

Iglesias, Enrique
Iglesias, Julio
La India (Linda Belle Caballero)
López, Jennifer
Martín, Ricky
Moreno, Rita
Rivera, Chita
Romay, Lina
Ronstadt, Linda
Selena (Selena Quintanilla Pérez)
Shakira
Vélez, Lisa

Social Activist

Alurista (Alberto Baltazar Urista)
Alvarado, Melba
Báez, Joan
Blades, Rubén
Casal, Lourdes
Chacón, Rafael
Chávez, César
Gillespie, Arlene F.
Gonzales, Rodolfo Corky
Gonzales, Sylvia Alicia
Hernández, Ester
Hernández-Ávila, Inés
Huerta, Dolores

Ibarra, Abdón
López, Yolanda
Molina, Gloria
Muñoz, Cecilia
Olmos, Edward James
Quintero, Sofía
Rodríguez, Cecilia
Sánchez, Elisa María
Sánchez, Sonia
Thomas, Piri
Tijerina, Reies López
Urdaneta, María-Luisa
Votaw, Carmen Delgado

Sportscaster

Carillo, Mary

Surgeon General

Novello, Antonia

Talk-Show Host

Cullum, Blanquita
Rivera, Geraldo
Saralegui, Cristina

Teacher

Alurista (Alberto Baltazar Urista)
Escalante, Jaime
Fuentes, Tina Guerrero
Gonzales, Rebecca

Martín, Patricia Preciado
Sánchez, Sonia
Simón, Laura Angélica
Solís, Octavio

Television Show Host

Betances, Samuel
Cutie, Alberto
Francisco, Don (Mario
    Kreutzberger)

Fuentes, Daisy
White, Vanna

Union Organizer

Chávez, César
Huerta, Dolores
Rodríguez, Arturo

Author Index

Subject and Key Word Index

About the Editors

DANIEL E. STANTON is a graduate student at the University of California, Berkeley.

EDWARD F. STANTON is the Chair of the Department of Spanish and Italian at the University of Kentucky, where he was the first Bingham Professor of the Humanities. He is the author of several books on Hispanic life and literature, including *Handbook of Spanish Popular Culture* (Greenwood, 1999).